TAKING THE

NUMB

OUT OF NUMBERS

Taking The Numb Out of Numbers

by

Don Fraser

Brendan Kelly Publishing Inc.
2122 Highview Drive
Burlington, Ontario
Canada   L7R 3X4
www.brendankellypublishing.com

Cover Design: Taisa Dorney

Illustrator: Taisa Dorney

Brendan Kelly Publishing Inc.
2122 Highview Drive
Burlington, Ontario
Canada L7R 3X4

ISBN 978-1-895997-08-8

ATTENTION EDUCATIONAL ORGANIZATIONS

Quantity discounts are available on bulk purchases of this book for educational
purposes or fund raising. For information, please contact:

Brendan Kelly Publishing Inc.
2122 Highview Drive
Burlington, Ontario
Canada L7R 3X4
www.brendankellypublishing.com

Telephone: (905) 335-3359   Fax: (905) 335-5104

Dedication

To my wife, Wendy, without whose loving encouragement this book would not have been written,

and

To the teachers and students from whom I've learned through the years.

Acknowledgments

I am pleased to express my gratitude to the following dedicated and caring teachers from the United States and Canada who took time to field test these activities.

Karin Berney
Karen Ramirez-Clark
Margaret Dalmer
Julie Howell
Shawn Lalonde
Suzanne Minutoli
Ahmed Mulla
Chad Soon
Peter Vogt
Sam Zomparelli

Julia Bynum
Nicki Cook
Lisa Friedberg
Denise Jackson
Father Bill Maloney
John Mirabelli
Nicole Ricketts
Tom Steinke
Susan Wallis

Radcliffe Campbell
Sandy Dainty
Sandy Hindy
Denise Johnson
Susan McNab
Audre Morgan
Michele Schlifstein
Sue Vitek
Ben Waxman

Our schools and our students are lucky to have keen teachers like you! Unfortunately restrictions on the book size have prevented us from including all the student work you submitted, but the student work that we were able to retain and your feedback have greatly enhanced the final product. Thanks again!

About the Author

Don Fraser is Professor Emeritus of Mathematics Education at the Ontario Institute for Studies in Education, University of Toronto, where he was a multiple winner of the prestigious *Teacher of the Year Award.*

His practical and innovative approaches to teaching at all levels from elementary to senior high school have won him international acclaim as one of North America's leading mathematics educators.

Professor Fraser's special gift for humor and for developing an instant rapport with audiences have made him one of the most internationally sought-after keynote and banquet speakers at mathematics conferences. He continues to deliver inspiring and motivational talks at conferences across this continent, ranging from California to Newfoundland and from Alaska to Florida.

Don's special flair for embedding mathematics in real-world contexts is evident in his highly successful publications: *Mathemagic, Newspaper Math, Sports Math,* and *Yesterday's Sports, Today's Math. Yesterday's Sports, Today's Math* is available from Dale Seymour/Cuisenaire Company of America in the U.S. and from Pearson Education in Canada. Don has also written educational materials for *The Toronto Star* and *USA TODAY.* In this revision of *Taking the Numb out of Numbers, Professor Fraser* has included more examples of newspaper clippings, current events, sports and entertainment to help you foster the development of number sense in contexts that are familiar to your students.

To contact Don directly email him at: dfraser@rogers.com

TABLE OF CONTENTS

TABLE OF CONTENTS

TAKING THE NUMB OUT OF NUMBERS... WHAT IT IS...

IT IS A COLLECTION OF:

• CRAZY, BUT REAL NEWSPAPER CLIPPINGS

• TOGETHER WITH INTERESTING QUESTIONS AND ACTIVITIES...

• ...THAT WILL HELP YOU DEVELOP SUCCESS AND CONFIDENCE IN WORKING WITH NUMBERS...

• ...CALLED "NUMERACY"...

• AND HIGHER ORDER THINKING SKILLS CALLED "PROBLEM SOLVING".

IT IS DIVIDED INTO SPECIAL SECTIONS EMPHASIZING:

COUNTING
SURVEYS
TALKING ABOUT PROBLEMS
ESTIMATION & MENTAL MATH
THE REASONABLE & THE UNREASONABLE
INDUCTIVE REASONING
WORD PROBLEMS
PROBLEMS WITHOUT ENOUGH INFORMATION
CALCULATORS

HOW TO USE TAKING THE NUMB OUT OF NUMBERS

If you open the book anywhere, you will find...

• A real newspaper clipping and an interesting question, activity or problem to be solved, (Reduced pages 38-41 are shown below.)...

SURVEY #1

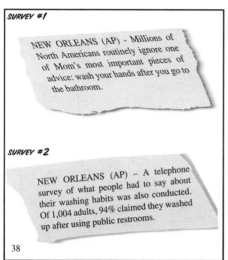

NEW ORLEANS (AP) - Millions of North Americans routinely ignore one of Mom's most important pieces of advice: wash your hands after you go to the bathroom.

SURVEY #2

NEW ORLEANS (AP) – A telephone survey of what people had to say about their washing habits was also conducted. Of 1,004 adults, 94% claimed they washed up after using public restrooms.

38

WHICH OF THE TWO SURVEYS DO YOU THINK IS CLOSER TO THE TRUTH?

WHY?

DOES THE SURVEY COUNT PEOPLE WHO WASH THEIR FACES?

39

...followed by a sample of student responses from across North America, and some *Thoughts and Theories* from the author.

SOME STUDENTS THOUGHT SURVEY #1 WAS CLOSER TO THE TRUTH...

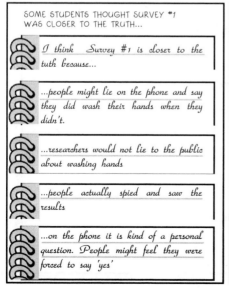

I think Survey #1 is closer to the truth because...

...people might lie on the phone and say they did wash their hands when they didn't.

...researchers would not lie to the public about washing hands

...people actually spied and saw the results

...on the phone it is kind of a personal question. People might feel they were forced to say 'yes'

... BUT THERE WERE OTHERS WHO THOUGHT SURVEY #2 WAS MORE ACCURATE.

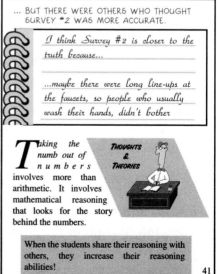

I think Survey #2 is closer to the truth because...

...maybe there were long line-ups at the faucets, so people who usually wash their hands, didn't bother

Taking the numb out of n u m b e r s involves more than arithmetic. It involves mathematical reasoning that looks for the story behind the numbers.

THOUGHTS & THEORIES

When the students share their reasoning with others, they increase their reasoning abilities!

41

11

HOW TO USE TAKING THE NUMB OUT OF NUMBERS

Here is a summary of strategies that will help you as you enjoy the exciting challenges in this book:

❶. **Read The Newspaper Clipping**

A weak reader is not a weak thinker. All can contribute to the solution.

If reading is a problem, work with a partner, or have the story read aloud or put the clipping on tape.

Talk about the clipping with others.

Learn the meaning of words which are new to you.

Relate the clipping to your own experience. Picture in your head what is described. Describe what is happening in your own words. Use your imagination and throw yourself into the story.

❷. **Read The Question or Problem Posed**

Try the question or problem before reading the student responses and the *Thoughts and Theories*. Then these will have more meaning!

Talk about the question with others. What does the question mean? Many questions can be interpreted in a variety of ways:
  • Listen to others.
  • Share your ideas.

What information would be needed to solve the problem? Is this information in the clipping? If not, how would you find this information?

❸. Apply a Problem Solving Strategy

Taking the numb out of numbers requires good problem solving strategies... Take your time. Problem solving is more like studying a poem than doing an arithmetic speed drill!

Many people become discouraged and give up if they don't see an immediate solution. Good problem solvers persevere and try again.

- Brainstorm. Talk to others. Discuss assumptions. Discuss strategies. If possible, use objects, draw a picture or diagram, or act out the situation.

- Take a risk – use trial-and-error or guess-and-check. A wrong guess may put you on the right path!

- Reduce the problem to a simpler related problem. If large numbers are bothering you, substitute smaller numbers until you see a solution unfolding!

- Make an organized list or table!

- Look for a pattern, use inductive reasoning! Use common sense!

❹. After Solving The Problem

After answering the question, question the answer.

Compare solutions with other people. Find someone who has made different assumptions. Do they have a different answer? Depending on the assumptions made, different answers are possible. That's why you are often asked to find *an* answer not *the* answer!

Find someone who has the same answer but who has solved the problem in a different way.

People who have *taken the numb out of numbers* often look at things in a variety of ways. Be open to different solutions.

WHAT DOES MATH TASTE LIKE?

FOR YOU, WHAT DOES MATH TASTE
LIKE? THINK ABOUT IT. WHY?

WRITE A FEW WORDS TO
DESCRIBE HOW MATH TASTES
TO YOU.

SHARE YOUR TASTE OF MATH
WITH FRIENDS AND FAMILY.

SOME ANSWERS GIVEN BY STUDENTS

Math tastes like sawdust — dry and gritty. You want to spit it out.

Math tastes like spinach. It doesn't taste very good, but it's good for you.

Math tastes like gum. At first it's good but then it loses its taste.

Math tastes like liver and onions, because I hate liver and I hate math.

Math tastes like an apple. First you have to wash it, then it's nice and shiny, then you take a bite and then you find there's a worm in it.

Math tastes like milk to me, because I drink milk every day and I do math every day. Milk helps me grow stronger and math helps my knowledge grow wider. But sometimes if you put milk in the refrigerator for a long time and don't drink it, it will turn into sour milk. If you don't do math and put it somewhere else, you won't learn anything new.

Math tastes like chocolate because at first when you look at chocolate it looks yucky, but then when you eat it, it melts in your mouth and tastes so good.

Students' answers to the question, "What does math taste like?" reveal much about their experiences and feelings about math. Unfortunately many people who have had a bad taste of math drop the subject at the earliest opportunity and lose out on many potential career choices!

With your help, young people can enjoy the pleasant taste of *Taking the Numb out of Numbers*. For them math will never taste the same again.

COUNTING

HERMAN® © Jim Unger/dist. by LaughingStock Licensing Inc.

10-15 © 1975 Jim Unger

"ONE."

IMAGINE THE COUNTING THAT LED TO THESE
STATEMENTS FROM REAL NEWSPAPER CLIPPINGS!

Every ear of corn has an even number of rows of kernels.

Manuel Oliveira has turned 567 foods into ice-cream flavors. These include onion, chili, spaghetti and spinach.

Ted Martin kept the hacky sack in the air for 48,825 consecutive kicks.

On Christmas Day 46,124 birds were counted.

Disney animators drew 6,469,952 spots for the film, "101 Dalmations".

One person once sent 62,824 Christmas cards.

COMPULSIVE COUNTING

Dear Ann Landers: Boy, do I have a dumb habit – and I don't know what possesses me to keep doing it or why.

I count everything I do! I count all my household chores and if I don't get through by a certain time I feel "uncomfortable" and "unfinished". I count how many dishes I wash, how many strokes it takes to brush my teeth and comb my hair. I even count the number of steps it takes to get from one place to another, although it doesn't matter and there's no reason to know.

Has anyone else ever written you about this nutty problem? I realize it's unusual and I'm embarrassed about it but I don't know who else to ask. I'm counting on you. Ha!

–CALGARY COUNTER

COUNTING SEEMS TO TAKE PLACE EVERYWHERE — IN SCHOOLS, IN STORES, IN HOMES, AS WELL AS AT THE PLAYGROUND AND ON THE STREET.

WHAT THINGS DO YOU COUNT?

FOR THE NEXT WEEK MAKE A LIST OF THINGS YOU COUNTED. SHARE YOUR LIST WITH FRIENDS.

MY LIST OF THINGS I COUNT

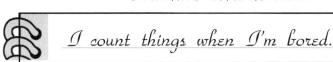

I count things when I'm bored.

I always count the cars on the freeway.

I count anything that is stacked up.

I count the Happy Faces on the bulletin board in Mrs. D's classroom.

Sometimes I count the steps it takes me to get home.

Sometimes I count on my fingers to do math.

I count when I get mad so the anger will go away.

At dinner, I'm the one who serves the napkins. And I couldn't just get a bunch of napkins. I have to count them because I don't want to go back to the kitchen.

I count my belches.

I love counting money.

Last year I was counting how many kids were in my class. First I counted 30. Then I counted 28.
After that I counted 32. Last I counted 32 again. So I thought it was 32. But my teacher counted 31.

C ounting by rote, calling out the numbers in order 1, 2, 3,... is not very useful.

On the other hand, counting rationally, which means counting objects or things, is a basic mathematics skill and is very useful! For example, how would a democracy work if we couldn't count the votes?

Relevance, interest and practice (R.I.P.) greatly increase the chance of learning taking place.

Mmmmmmmmmmm...

THE REMARKABLE HUMMINGBIRD

The hummingbird is quite remarkable! It flaps its wings 3000 times in a minute. Survival is a constant struggle to take in energy, by sipping nectar, faster than it burns energy while flying.

As a result the hummingbird eats about every six minutes. In migration the birds can fly 800 km non-stop across the Gulf of Mexico in 26 hours.

Did you know that, while flying, a hummingbird's heart beats 1200 times each minute?!

ACCORDING TO THE ARTICLE, THE HUMMINGBIRD FLAPS ITS WINGS 3000 TIMES IN A MINUTE. TO FIND OUT WHAT THIS *REALLY* MEANS, WE WILL COMPARE *YOUR* FLAPPING ABILITY WITH THE HUMMINGBIRD'S.

❶. AFTER DECIDING WHAT A "FLAP" IS, ESTIMATE OR GUESS HOW MANY TIMES YOU CAN "FLAP" YOUR ARMS IN 10 SECONDS.

❷. WORK WITH TWO OTHER PEOPLE TO *COUNT* HOW MANY "FLAPS" YOU CAN ACTUALLY DO IN 10 SECONDS.
THERE ARE THREE ROLES — FLAPPER, TIMER & COUNTER
EACH PERSON SHOULD HAVE A CHANCE TO PLAY ALL THREE ROLES.

❸. AS A GROUP DECIDE HOW YOUR FLAPPING ABILITY COMPARES TO A HUMMINGBIRD'S.

STUDENTS REPORT RESULTS

Eric

Guess   10

He really got 23

Vanessa

Estimate   14

Vanessa flapped 25

Teresa flapped 26 times in 10 seconds

In one minute that would be 156 flaps

$$\begin{array}{r} \overset{3}{2}6 \\ \times 6 \\ \hline 156 \end{array}$$

Estimates:	First try	Second try
Lisa Chen ...7 times	19	27
Carlos S.... 20 times	21	35
Victor O. ...10 times	23	27

Human beings are pretty slow in flapping their arms. The hummingbirds are about 14 times faster than us!

Do you usually get excited when you write down two numbers? Probably not! However, that's all the students did in this activity, and they really got excited.

Students find it much more interesting to work with numbers that they have generated through an activity, rather than with numbers copied from a text.

With these numbers, we can ask all sorts of stimulating questions that lead to the arithmetic operations – addition, subtraction, multiplication and division. Students can explore the concept of *average*, and graph the results of this activity.

To compare our human results with the hummingbird's we need a common time interval. One way to find this is to multiply the number of human flaps by 6 to see how many flaps one might do in one minute. Compare this result with the hummingbird's 3000 flaps. Another way to compare is to determine how many flaps per second were achieved on average by the students. The hummingbird does 50!

For more math and more excitement, vary the time given for the students to "flap". Notice the fatigue factor. For real excitement have a "flap-off" to find the best "flapper" in the class or at home!

TWO SCOOPS OF RAISINS

The Latest Scoop on Raisins

How many scoops of raisins in a box of Raisin Bran?

Not having a scoop handy (whatever that is!), your investigative reporter tried to answer an easier question – How many raisins in a box of Raisin Bran?

Upon counting the raisins in an 800-gram box of Raisin Bran, it was discovered that there were 760 raisins in total!

The company who makes the cereal claims the ratio of raisins to bran by weight is about 30% – even though the number of raisins will vary from box to box.

Meanwhile, back at the scoop, Lorne McCuish is upset with the ad that claims there are "two scoops of raisins in a box of *Raisin Bran*." McCuish says, "The television commercial uses a very large scoop that creates a misconception in the public mind."

However, Miriam Armstrong, spokesperson for the consumer and corporate affairs department says that the company does not say how big the scoop is and is, therefore, not breaking any law by promising two scoops in their advertisement.

TAKE AN 800-GRAM BOX OF *KELLOGG'S RAISIN BRAN.*

HOW MANY RAISINS DO YOU THINK ARE IN THIS BOX?

OPEN THE BOX AND COUNT THE RAISINS.

(OOPS, ONE STUDENT MISREAD THE INSTRUCTIONS AND TOOK AN 800-KG BOX!)

HERE'S WHAT ONE TEACHER WROTE IN HER JOURNAL

I really enjoyed being part of the Raisin Bran experiment, and so did my students. They were so excited to hear that another class at another school was doing the same experiment and that they were going to share results.

Most of the students' initial guesses were extremely low, e.g. 50 raisins. I wonder why? How big do they think raisins are? If they think they are really big, then maybe they think they will take up more room in the box. As well, some students didn't know what a raisin is. Many students responded with a gasp when told that raisins are dried grapes. Maybe they would have better predictions if I had shown them a raisin before they made their guesses.

— Nicki Cook

NICKI'S STUDENTS WROTE THE FOLLOWING

We did an experiment on Raisin Bran. Each group got two bowls. One of the bowls in each group had Raisin Bran in it and the other bowl was empty. Then we picked out the raisins and put them in the empty bowl. All the groups went to the carpet and we added up all the raisins.

After, four kids wrote a letter to Mr. Zomparelli's class and they said what we did with Raisin Bran and also how much was in the box of Raisin Bran. We found that they had 492 raisins in their box, and we had 630 raisins in our box. We learned that every box has a different number of raisins. We think the two scoops are different sizes.

Mr. Zomparelli's kids ate the rasins and gave the bran to the birds. In our class everyone guessed how much there would be in the box, and the closest was Alisha. She guessed 500. That is what we did on Raisin Bran.

—Alisha, Kojo, and Naseer and all the students in Ms. Cook's grade 4 class!

C ounting large numbers of objects is not easy, even for adults. Most students find it helpful when counting a large number of objects to place the objects in groups of 10 and then combine ten groups of 10 into a large group of 100. An advantage of this procedure is that it makes it easier to check the answer.

Students who have experienced large numbers in counting situations display a superior understanding of the meanings of these numbers.

Relating arithmetic to the "real world" of the student is an important step towards *taking the numb out of numbers*!

In this investigation, Ms. Cook has cleverly linked numeracy and literacy. As the students write about their experiences and those of the other class, they come to realize that the scoop is not a standard unit and that different scoops may hold different numbers of raisins. She has also recorded her own observations in a journal, indirectly communicating to the students that she regards the maintenance of a journal as an important part of the investigation process.

Communication is an important aspect of mathematics. By sharing our ideas with others, we clarify the ideas in our own mind.

By permission of Johnny Hart and Creators Syndicate, Inc.

SURVEYS

USA SNAPSHOTS®

A look at statistics that shape our lives

Favorite ways to wash pets

Shower with owner **3%**

No preference/ don't know **11%**

Professionally **25%**

Tub **33%**

28% Garden hose

Source: Teledyne Water Pik

By Anne R. Carey and Web Bryant, USA TODAY

The average person in the USA has seen the movie *Star Wars* in theaters or on TV 6.7 times.

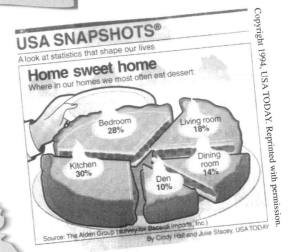

USA SNAPSHOTS®
A look at statistics that shape our lives

Home sweet home
Where in our homes we most often eat dessert:

Kitchen 30%
Bedroom 28%
Living room 18%
Dining room 14%
Den 10%

Source: The Alden Group (survey for Bacardi Imports, Inc.)
By Cindy Hall and Julie Stacey, USA TODAY

Copyright 1994, USA TODAY. Reprinted with permission.

One in ten Californians owns a convertible.

80% of people count the number of packages of the person in front of them in an express check-out line.

On what night would you like to see Monday Night Football?

Monday 69%
Friday............................12%
Thursday 6%
Wednesday...................... 5%
Saturday 4%
Sunday............................ 3%
Tuesday 1%

ARE YOU SERIOUS?

SOME HEADLINES FROM THE NEWSPAPER...

1

Men Make Up Only 15% Of All Grocery Shoppers Now!

2

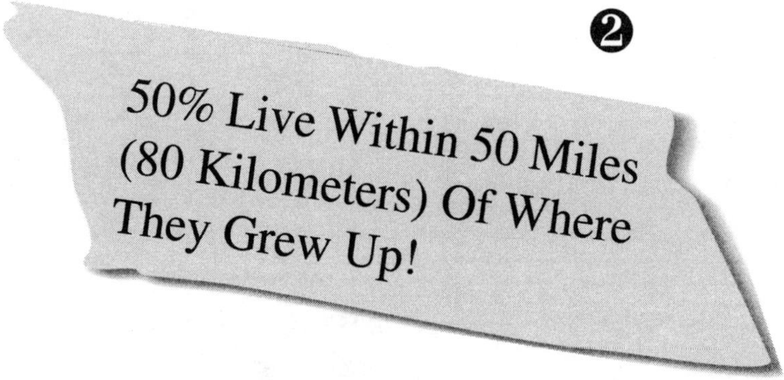

50% Live Within 50 Miles (80 Kilometers) Of Where They Grew Up!

3

32% Never Go To The Movies!

DO YOU BELIEVE THESE HEADLINES?

FOR EACH OF THE THREE HEADLINES, CHOOSE A, B, OR C, WHERE...

A means DEFINITELY TRUE!
B means MAYBE TRUE, MAYBE NOT TRUE. I'M NOT SURE
C means NO WAY! IT'S NOT TRUE!

CHOOSE ONE OF THE HEADLINES AND CONDUCT YOUR OWN SURVEY.
RECORD YOUR RESULTS.

DISCUSS WITH FRIENDS OR FAMILY THE REASONS WHY YOUR RESULTS WERE THE SAME OR DIFFERENT FROM THE NEWSPAPER HEADLINE.

MANY DIFFERENT SURVEYS WERE DONE BY STUDENTS.

1

I think this is true because my father never goes shopping. Some people may have different points of view but this is mine.

Studies show that when I went to Shop Rite there were only 12 men in the supermarket.

I stood outside of Edwards supermarket and counted 100 people walking into Edwards and about 25% were men. About 10% shopped alone and the other 15% shopped with a woman. This survey was taken on a Saturday afternoon when a lot of men are home. I do notice when I shop with my mom on a weekday morning that there are definitely more women than men.

2

Not true because in my family out of 5 of us, 2 do not live within 50 miles from where they grew up. Grandpa was born and grew up in Jamaica Queens, but now lives in Ozone Park.
Mom grew up in Ozone Park and now lives in North Bellmore.
My brother, sister and I are growing up in North Bellmore.

No way - I got this by asking 20 people. I went into my mom's phonebook and called some numbers. I also went to my friend's house and asked some people. I also just walked around the block and anyone I saw, I asked.

Suppose you wanted to find out something about ALL the people in your country. It would be impossible to ask everybody. So what you can do is to ask SOME people and hope that their answers express the views of everybody. This is called a *survey*!

What better way to learn about a survey than by taking one yourself! Many things have to be considered...

> Whom do you survey?
> How many people do you survey?
> What do you ask?
> Is the question clear?
> How will you organize the answers?
> What conclusions can you make?

By taking their own surveys, these students have challenged the truth of the newspaper headlines. They have questioned what they have read. Testing the validity of published statements is an important life skill. The fact that an article contains numbers doesn't necessarily imply its claims are true.

A DIFFERENCE OF OPINION

SURVEY #1

NEW ORLEANS (AP) - Millions of North Americans routinely ignore one of Mom's most important pieces of advice: wash your hands after you go to the bathroom.

This unsettling item of news was gathered in the only way possible – by actually watching what people do (or don't do) in public washrooms.

Researchers hid in stalls or pretended to comb their hair while observing 6,333 men and women do their business in five cities recently.

The survey found that 74% of women and only 61% of men wash after using the toilet.

Dr. Michael Osterholm, the Minnesota state epidemiologist concluded that "hand washing has become all but a lost art."

SURVEY #2

NEW ORLEANS (AP) - A telephone survey of what people had to say about their washing habits was also conducted. Of 1,004 adults, 94% claimed they washed up after using public restrooms.

WHICH OF THE TWO SURVEYS DO YOU THINK IS CLOSER
TO THE TRUTH?

WHY?

DOES THE SURVEY COUNT
PEOPLE WHO WASH THEIR FACE?

SOME STUDENTS THOUGHT SURVEY #1 WAS CLOSER
TO THE TRUTH...

I think Survey #1 is closer to the truth because...

...people might lie on the phone and say they did wash their hands when they didn't.

...researchers would not lie to the public about washing hands.

...people actually spied and saw the results.

...on the phone it is kind of a personal question. People might feel they were forced to say 'yes'.

...some people would be embarrassed to say 'no' on the phone.

BUT THERE WERE OTHERS WHO THOUGHT SURVEY #2
WAS MORE ACCURATE.

I think Survey #2 is closer to the truth because...

...maybe there were long line-ups at the faucets, so people who usually wash their hands, didn't bother.

Taking the numb out of numbers involves more than arithmetic. It involves mathematical reasoning that looks for the story behind the numbers.

When the students share their reasoning with others, they increase their reasoning abilities!

THAT'S HARD TO BELIEVE !

HERE ARE THE RESULTS OF TWO SURVEYS...
THE ONLY THING MISSING IS THE NUMBERS!

❶

The average American buys ⬭ pairs of sunglasses in a lifetime.

❷

⬭% of drivers have eaten a meal while driving.

WHAT DO YOU THINK ARE THE TWO MISSING NUMBERS?

USE ARITHMETIC AND COMMON SENSE TO EXPLAIN WHY YOU CHOSE THESE ANSWERS.

WRITE YOUR EXPLANATION SO THAT OTHERS WILL UNDERSTAND YOUR REASONING.

❶

I have had 20 pairs of sunglasses in 12 years. So if every 12 years you buy 20 pairs, then you will end up with 120 pairs of sunglasses by the time you are 72.

SUNGLASSES	
YOUNG	10
ELEMENTARY	5
TEENAGER	20
ADULT	20
SENIOR	25
TOTAL	80

I think 80 is correct because when you are young you would get all the Barbie and Superman sunglasses. When you are in elementary you get them to be cool. When you are a teenager you still want to be cool and you get the wrap arounds. When you are an adult you need them when you drive. Senior citizens have bad eyesight.

❷

DIFFERENT SITUATIONS WERE CONSIDERED BY DIFFERENT STUDENTS...

Breakfast, lunch and dinner – Most people eat breakfast while driving, but fewer do at lunch and dinner, because most drivers are at their destination.

It takes 20 minutes to eat a meal. Therefore, for trips under 20 minutes they don't eat a meal while driving. When people are going on vacation, they usually pack meals.

When I am looking out the window of our car I see 25% eating because they are rushed.

I think that old drivers and really new drivers probably don't eat. This is because new drivers aren't sure of themselves and old drivers can't see so well so they can't pay attention to a burger.

All my relatives have eaten a meal while driving. My dad is a trucker so he eats all the time while driving.

I think that 33% of drivers had eaten a meal while driving — 30% morning drivers, 2% afternoon drivers and 1% evening drivers.

Did adding these percents lead to a logical answer?

According to the survey…

- The average American buys 31 pairs of sunglasses in a lifetime.

- 42% of drivers have eaten a meal while driving.

Many students dislike math because they are afraid of making a mistake. Guessing at the result of a survey is something that all students can do and enjoy!

Playing with numbers in this way helps reduce the fear of mathematics, and paves the way to success – the best motivator.

TV OR NOT TV ? – THAT IS THE QUESTION

WHAT IS YOUR FAVORITE TV PROGRAM? SURVEY YOUR CLASS TO SEE IF THEY AGREE.

BELOW ARE THE TOP 15 PROGRAMS FOR THE FIRST WEEK IN DECEMBER, 2006.

Rank	Show	Network	No. of Viewers (millions)
1	Grey's Anatomy	ABC	24.0
2	NCIS	CBS	18.0
3	Criminal Minds	CBS	17.9
4	Deal or No Deal	NBC	17.9
5	House	FOX	17.3
6	CSI:Miami	CBS	17.1
7	The OC	FOX	16.5
8	CSI:NY	CBS	16.4
9	CSI	CBS	16.1
10	Survivor: Cook Islands	CBS	15.6
10	Heroes	NBC	15.6
12	Two and a Half Men	CBS	15.5
13	Sunday Night Football	NBC	15.4
14	Law & Order:SVU	NBC	14.6
15	Without a Trace	CBS	14.3

HERE ARE SOME STUDENT-MADE QUESTIONS...

How many people watched *Deal or No Deal*?

What show had 14.3 million viewers?

What was the most popular *CSI* show?

How many more people watched *Grey's Anatomy* than *House*?

Explain how you could use the chart to find the most popular network? Can you think of another way to do this?

Using the shows and the number of viewers we can make equations ...

Criminal Minds + The OC = NCIS + CSI:NY

$$17.9 + 16.5 = 18.0 + 16.4$$

CSI — Law & Order:SVU = CSI:Miami — Heroes

$$16.1 — 14.6 = 17.1 — 15.6$$

See how many equations you can make.

THE NEWSPAPER **USA TODAY** IS A WEEKLY SOURCE FOR TV RATINGS

Use integers to describe the change in rank of your favorite TV program from week to week.

For Example: Last week CSI Miami was ranked #2. This week it is #6. The integer −4 shows the change. Use positive integers to show improvement and negative integers to show a decline. What does the integer 0 mean?

A low rating means not many people are watching the program. Advertisers don't want to pay the networks "big bucks" to sponsor a low rated program. Maybe that is why some of the lower rated programs are no longer on TV!

Often students do word problems by shuffling the numbers around until they get the answer in the back of the textbook. By creating their own word problems the students become much more involved – using their thinking, literacy, and math skills as well as their common sense.

Student-created questions also provide a realistic assessment of the students' level of understanding. What a nice ready-made package of questions for the teacher to use with other classes!

Most students are very interested in television. Realizing that one of their interests connects with math is a big step towards *taking the numb out of numbers*.

In the words of visionary Seymour Papert,

> *...First, relate what is new and to be learned to something you already know. Second, take what is new and make it your own. Make something new with it, play with it, build with it.*

> – Mindstorms: Children, Computers and Powerful Ideas, 1980

SWEATPANTS OR WHAT ?

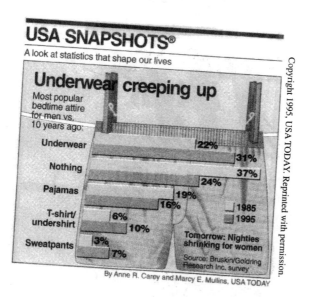

USA SNAPSHOTS®
A look at statistics that shape our lives

Underwear creeping up

Most popular bedtime attire for men vs. 10 years ago:

Underwear	22% / 31%
Nothing	37% / 24%
Pajamas	19% / 16%
T-shirt/ undershirt	6% / 10%
Sweatpants	3% / 7%

☐ 1985
☐ 1995

Tomorrow: Nighties shrinking for women

Source: Bruskin/Goldring Research Inc. survey

By Anne R. Carey and Marcy E. Mullins, USA TODAY

USA SNAPSHOTS®
A look at statistics that shape our lives

Nighties shrinking

Most popular bedtime attire for women vs. 10 years ago:

Nightie/ nightgown	53% / 40%
Pajamas	19% / 25%
T-shirts	3% / 14%
Nightshirt	3% / 6%
Sweatpants	1% / 7%
Nothing	6% / 6%

☐ 1985
☐ 1995

Source: Bruskin/Goldring Research Inc. survey

By Anne R. Carey and Marcy E. Mullins, USA TODAY

TURN THE GRAPHS AND THE STATS INTO A NEWS
STORY.

SOME SUGGESTED TITLES ARE.....

" WHAT PEOPLE WEAR TO BED HAS CHANGED
THROUGH THE YEARS."

" THE DIFFERENCE BETWEEN MEN AND WOMEN"

" WHAT REALLY SURPRISES ME"

I think more men wear underwear now because work starts earlier so they need to just put clothes on and get to work.

Fewer men used to wear underwear back then because it was improper.

Now you can get cool boxers like Looney Tunes and Santa Claus boxers.

I think the men who wear pyjamas is fewer than in 1985 because only a few stores sell pyjamas now.

More men are wearing underwear now because it is hotter in America than 10 years ago.

Nightgowns are popular because they are comfortable.

Older women wear cotton nightgowns because they are not as warm to sleep in during the summer.

The biggest change for women over the 10 years has been more T-shirts.

In 1985 most men preferred to wear nothing at bedtime. Is it because they couldn't afford underwear? Maybe! But what we found out was that it's not that they could not afford it. It is just that more people felt comfortable wearing nothing. As for women, they are more conservative!

A picture is worth 1000 words only if you understand it!

Students need practice in order to understand what a graph is saying. Talking and writing about the graph speeds up everyone's understanding.

Many graphs raise questions as well as give answers...
For example in this case questions have come up such as,

What if you wore a T-shirt and sweatpants?

What if you don't do the same thing all the time?

What question would be asked to arrive at this graph ?

An important step in *taking the numb out of numbers* is to read and understand graphs as well as understand their limitations.

People who have *taken the numb out of numbers* are able to take numbers from the graph, interpret them, play with them, compare them, and point out some new meaning which was not obvious from the graph. These "real-life" skills constitute an important part of what is now *graph literacy.*

Talk About It

NUBBIN

Reprinted with special permission of King Features Syndicate

IN THIS PART OF THE BOOK, THE EMPHASIS IS ON TAKING A NEWSPAPER CLIPPING AND *TALKING ABOUT IT!*

Robber starts lawsuit after paralyzing fall

The Daily Recorder reports that the Assemblyman, Alister McAlister, is introducing legislation to prevent thieves from suing the owner of property they are trespassing upon.

Well, in Redding, a burglar was paralyzed after falling through a skylight of a school he was breaking into. He sued for $3 million charging that the school failed to warn him the skylight was unsafe.

The first year he got $260,000 in an out-of-court settlement plus $1200 a month for life.

YOU BE THE JUDGE!
IS THE SETTLEMENT FAIR?
TALK ABOUT IT

Character studies

In a test of Europeans' honesty, journalists from *The Reader's Digest* scattered 10 wallets in each of 20 cities. People returned 116 of the billfolds, which included the equivalent of about $60 in cash, a name, address and phone number and family snapshots. "The most surprising thing was that you could not tell from appearances what people would do with the wallets," said William Echikson, one of the study's co-authors. "I saw grandmothers steal them and often impoverished immigrants return them."

WOULD YOU RETURN THE BILLFOLD?
TALK ABOUT IT

WE'RE GOING TO DISNEY WORLD

BOSTON – Two sisters, 15 and 14, and a friend, 13, were arraigned on charges of stealing the sisters' retired grandmother's life savings to finance a trip to Disney World. Over three days, the girls spent all but $8,100 of the $26,500 they took from Beatrice Jones, 63, police say.

INTERNET

EXPLORATION

TRAVEL TO DISNEY WORLD – ON THE INTERNET!

IT WON'T COST YOUR GRANDMOTHER A PENNY.

EXPLORE SOME OF THE SPECIAL FEATURES OFFERED ON THE DISNEY WORLD HOME PAGE AT THIS WEBSITE: **http://www.disney.com/**

HOW MUCH MONEY DID THE GIRLS HAVE LEFT AFTER
THEIR ADVENTURE?

TALK ABOUT IT...

IF YOU WERE A JUDGE, HOW WOULD YOU
DEAL WITH THESE TEENAGERS?

THE GIRLS HAD $8,100 LEFT AFTER THEIR ADVENTURE.

TALKING ABOUT IT, STUDENTS SHOWED NO SYMPATHY:

Put them in jail for stealing from an old woman.

Have them confess themselves to their grandmother. Don't put them in Juvenile Hall, but let them do some sort of community work to pay back the stolen money.

It all depends on whether the grandmother wants to press charges or if she wants to take care of the problem.

I would punish them because if you let them go they will just do it again because they'll think you won't do anything about it.

See a counsellor once a week.

I can understand the urge to want to go to Disney World but to take money by force from your own blood is cruel and rude.

The answer, \$8,100, required no arithmetic to find! Close to 50% of the students tested gave the wrong answer. Most said

$$\$26,500 - \$8,100 = \$18,400$$

....an example of good arithmetic, **but the wrong answer!**

Taking the numb out of numbers involves more than arithmetic – it involves problem solving as well!

Many students see problems like this simply as hidden arithmetic questions– not as problems to solve. Consequently they feel they must get quick answers and so they often jump to the wrong conclusion. Careful reading and understanding of the clipping takes time. The phrase "all but \$8,100" should be expressed by the students in their own words.

A good problem solving strategy would be to act out the story using smaller numbers, e.g.\$26 and \$8, then students will notice the importance of the words "all but \$8".

COUGARS OR KIDS ?

Cougar kills mother

In April, a 40-year-old woman was mauled to death by a cougar on a mountain trail in northern California, leaving her two children, aged 8 and 5 motherless. After the cougar was tracked down and killed a week later, Folsom City Zoo set up a trust fund for the cougar's cub. As of mid-May, the cub's fund had received $21,000, vs. $9,000 for a trust fund established for the woman's children.

❶. HOW MUCH MONEY WAS IN THE CUB'S TRUST FUND?

❷. HOW MUCH MONEY WAS IN THE CHILDREN'S TRUST FUND?

❸. HOW MUCH MONEY WOULD HAVE TO BE ADDED TO THE CHILDREN'S TRUST FUND TO MATCH THE CUB'S TRUST FUND?

TALK ABOUT IT...

TO WHICH FUND WOULD YOU CHOOSE TO DONATE – THE CHILDREN'S FUND OR THE CUB'S FUND? WHY?

THE ANSWERS ARE ...
❶. $21,000   ❷. $9,000   ❸. $12,000

IN TALKING ABOUT IT, MANY STUDENTS CHOSE THE
CHILDREN'S FUND BECAUSE...

They need money to help their foster parents care for them.

The children would be sad and troubled.

They would need money for the funeral.

We can take care of the cougar, but the cougar can't take care of us.

The cub already gets enough money from the zoo's entrance fund.

The kids need money to go to college.

The cougar was the one who started it.

I would donate to the cub's fund because they are becoming extinct.

 The cub's fund because they are cute.

 Maybe both because the cougars need somewhere to live and the children need clothes and toys.

If students don't understand the meaning of the words in a clipping, then they have little hope of solving the math problems. It is important to take the time needed to understand the words in a newsclip. Talking about the clipping with others helps!

Students who did not thoroughly understand the clipping, noted the word 'added' in question 3 and gave an incorrect answer – $30,000.

BABY BOOM

Parents brace for life with septuplets

DES MOINES, Iowa (AP-Reuters) – Three hundred and fifty diapers every week. That's what Bobbi and Kenny McCaughey will be changing as soon as their newborn septuplets are out of the hospital and in their Carlisle, Iowa home.

The septuplets were delivered by caesarean section November 19, at the Iowa Methodist Medical Center and both parents are happy that Kenneth, Alexis, Natalie, Kelsey, Brandon, Nathaniel, and Joel are all healthy.

But you can understand why their joy is a little restrained. The babies' birth produced conflicting emotions for both parents.

ON AVERAGE HOW MANY DIAPERS WOULD EACH BABY USE EACH WEEK?

TALK ABOUT IT...

SUPPOSE YOU ARE AN OLDER BROTHER OR SISTER OF THE SEPTUPLETS, WHAT MIGHT BE SOME OF YOUR 'CONFLICTING EMOTIONS'?

IN TALKING ABOUT IT, THESE ARE SOME OF THE
"CONFLICTING EMOTIONS" FELT BY STUDENTS....

I would be jealous because the babies would get most of the attention.

I would be tired helping my mom with the babies.

All that crying, day and night

Wouldn't be enough money for good clothes.

Pretty hard trying to change 350 diapers a week.

Having to set a good example

Having to treat all of them the same way

I'd be happy because I like babies, but with seven babies at one time I would be doing nothing but baby-sitting — no time for anything else.

My emotions would be left out.

Put them up for adoption.

Scared because we'd have to look after seven kids who might be kidnapped.

WHAT A RANGE OF FEELINGS IN A SINGLE CLASSROOM!

Most students had no problem getting the answer (350 ÷ 7 or 50 diapers used by each baby). As a matter of fact, students suspected they had made a mistake because the solution seemed so easy. What does this say about their confidence in solving math problems? People who have *taken the numb out of numbers* expect to be able to solve a problem!

> Creating a positive environment in which students are motivated to solve problems and demonstrate confidence in their ability to reach correct solutions, is an important first step in fostering the development of problem solving skills.

ESTIMATION & MENTAL MATH

Bed Sheets too short, prisoner dies in escape bid

MONTREAL (CP) – One prisoner died and another was injured when they tried to escape from a detention center using knotted bed sheets that were too short.

Bungee cord was too long

ARVADA, Colo. (AP) – A man killed during a bungee jump was fastened to a cord that was 70 feet too long, an investigator says.

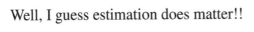

Well, I guess estimation does matter!!

The Macarena

No one is happier to see the macarena fade in popularity than the folks who make a living delivering pizzas. According to a Domino's pizza study, approximately 1,500 households last year were playing the macarena when a Domino's delivery person arrived. And in at least 459 cases, Domino's employees were told that the size of their tip depended on how successfully they joined in the dance.

Considering 500/1500 we realize that this situation probably affected fewer than 1/3 of the delivery people.

Sesame Seeds

McDonald's has put 2,492,000,000,000 sesame seeds on 14,000,000,000 Big Macs over 25 years!

By mentally dividing 2,800 by 14, we learn that each Big Mac has about 200 sesame seeds.

He walks 15 km – on his knees for true love

SAO PAULO (Reuter) – A love-struck Brazilian artist, distraught over the breakup of a four-year relationship with his girlfriend, shuffled 15 kilometers on his knees in a bid to win back her love.

She still rejected him.

Shuffling along with pieces of car tire tied to his kneecaps and cheered on by motorists and passersby, 21-year-old Marcio da Silva took 14 hours to complete his journey from Praia Grande to Santos.

When he arrived at her home, 19-year-old Katia de Nascimento had left to avoid seeing him.

A little mental math shows that Marcio crawled at a little over one kilometer per hour!

THE BEST DEAL IN TOWN

AS SCHOOL STARTS EACH FALL, STORES ARE STOCKED WITH PACKAGES OF THREE-HOLED PAPER. OFTEN THE PACKAGES ARE SOLD AT SPECIAL 'BACK TO SCHOOL' SALE PRICES.

THESE ARE THE SALE PRICES FOUND BY SOME MIDDLE SCHOOL STUDENTS WHO TRAVELED TO THEIR SCHOOL FROM ALL OVER THE CITY.

Number of Sheets	Cost
200	$1.99
200	$2.99
400	$3.99
400	$2.49
200	$0.99
300	$1.99
400	$2.89
400	$1.99
300	$2.19
400	$2.69
400	$1.20

WHICH IS THE BEST DEAL IN TOWN?   WHY?

NAOMI'S PHOTOCOPY PAPER 400 SHEETS FOR $2.89

JAKE'S SCHOOL SUPPLIES 300 SHEETS FOR $2.19

MOST STUDENTS AGREED THAT THE BEST DEAL IN
TOWN IS 400 SHEETS FOR $1.20.

With a calculator I found...

Number of Sheets	Cost (cents)	Number of Sheets for 1 cent
200	199	1.005025126
200	299	0.668896321
400	399	1.002506266
400	249	1.606425703
200	99	2.02020202
300	199	1.507537688
400	289	1.384083045
400	199	2.010050251
300	219	1.369863014
400	269	1.486988848
400	120	3.333333333

The Best Deal by far is 400 sheets for $1.20, over 3 sheets for 1 cent!

U sing a calculator and doing 11 calculations is too much work. People who *take the numb out of numbers* look for the easy way!

An easier solution, without the need for a calculator, is to find the best deal on 200 sheets, the best deal on 300 sheets, and the best deal on 400 sheets and then compare the results.

Simple comparisons yield these best deals:
200 sheets $0.99
300 sheets $1.99
400 sheets $1.20

By observation, '400 sheets' is a better deal than '200 sheets' because '400 sheets' does not cost double '200 sheets. Also, comparing '400 sheets' and '300 sheets', with '400 sheets' you get more for less! So 400 sheets for $1.20 is *the best deal in town* (as long as the store is close to you!)

To put the discussion in a real world context, it is important to discuss the idea that the cheapest per sheet cost is not always the best deal. If the sheets are so thin that you can use only one side, then buying this kind of paper may be *false economy*. Such considerations must be included in any purchase decision.

Furthermore, using a calculator is not always the easiest way to solve a problem. Sorting, estimating, and mental math, along with common sense remain important math tools.

Dog—Gone

LYNDON, Vt. (UPI) -Barry Waldner a 22-year-old college student has broken the world's record for eating hot dogs.

After eating 21 hot dogs in four minutes and 15 seconds and breaking the old record by 32 seconds, he said: "Us off-campus people don't get much to eat.".

❶. ABOUT HOW MANY MINUTES DID BARRY TAKE TO EAT 21 HOT DOGS?

❷. AT THIS SPEED, HOW MANY HOT DOGS COULD BARRY EAT IN 1 HOUR ?

❸. IF YOU USED BARRY'S ACTUAL TIME OF FOUR MINUTES AND 15 SECONDS TO EAT 21 HOT DOGS, WOULD BARRY EAT MORE OR FEWER HOT DOGS THAN THE ANSWER TO QUESTION ❷. EXPLAIN.

TALK ABOUT IT...

DO YOU THINK BARRY COULD ACTUALLY EAT THAT MANY HOT DOGS IN ONE HOUR?

HERE IS A SET OF CORRECT ANSWERS.

❶. 4 minutes ("about" calls for rounding)

❷. 15 × 21 = 315 hot dogs

❸. The answer would be smaller. He would eat fewer hot dogs because he is taking longer to eat each one.

STUDENTS SUPPLIED A RANGE OF ANSWERS TO QUESTION ❷ — SOME CORRECT...

4	21
8	42
12	63
16	84
20	105
24	126
28	147
32	168
36	189
40	210
44	231
48	252
52	273
56	294
60	315

He could eat 315 hot dogs.

$$
\begin{array}{r}
15 \\
\times\ 21 \\
\hline
15 \\
300 \\
\hline
315
\end{array}
$$

```
   21
 + 60
   81   He could eat 81 hot dogs.
```

```
 60 + 21 = 81

 81 × 4 = 324 hot dogs
```

```
 21 × 60 = 1260 hot dogs
```

In response to Talk About It, a student wrote, "No way, Jose!"

Some students understood the clipping, some didn't. The organized list technique was a very good problem solving strategy. It took more time, but showed that the student knew how to *take the numb out of numbers.*

Students must be encouraged to discuss what the numbers mean when they are combined. Don't let the need for extra time be a problem. Speed doesn't matter in problem solving.

Multiplying by 15 is a nice thing to do mentally, i.e., in your head. First multiply by 10, then take half of this and add the results.

e.g. $15 \times 21 = 10 \times 21 = 210$....half of 210 is 105
So the answer is $210 + 105 = 315$

Multiplying by 15 mentally is a useful skill to have when working out a 15% tip in a fancy restaurant!

A BIG CROWD

Police say "simple math" confirms 75,000 at rally

A police crowd estimate of 75,000 for Saturday's Day of Action parade and rally at Queen's Park is based on "pure, simple math," says Stan Belza, the officer responsible for the count. Organizers of the rally claim there were 250,000 present. To get their estimate police measured the area from Queen's Park to College Street to come up with 27,000 square meters able to be occupied by crowds. The police also estimated that at most four people could occupy each square meter. According to Belza, "At the parade, they did not have four people per square meter crammed into every possible square meter."

❶. GIVEN THE INFORMATION IN THE BOXED PART OF THE CLIPPING, WHAT IS THE LARGEST NUMBER OF PEOPLE THAT COULD BE AT THE RALLY?

❷. USE TAPE TO CREATE A SQUARE METER ON THE GROUND.
SEE HOW MANY PEOPLE YOU CAN CROWD INSIDE A SQUARE METER.
IF YOU USE THIS NUMBER OF PEOPLE, NOT FOUR, WHAT WOULD BE YOUR ANSWER TO QUESTION **❶**.

1. The most number of people who could be at the rally was

   $4 \times 27{,}000 = 108{,}000$ people.

2. Many groups were surprised to be able to squeeze 9 people into a square meter In that case, the answer would be

   $9 \times 27{,}000 = 243{,}000$ people

It is interesting that for an increase of one person in each square meter the crowd size increases by 27,000 people! Many students felt that this was not a good basis for a crowd size estimate. Different people would come and go over the duration of the rally.

Others noted the word *parade* and talked about different ways of counting the numbers in a parade. They took into account the width of the road, the number of people passing a vantage point every few seconds, the time the parade lasted, etc.

Boxing a relevant part of the article decreases the amount that students must read and increases the chances of success for students for whom reading is sometimes overwhelming. However, many students will read the whole article if it is interesting!

Remember, a weak reader doesn't mean a weak thinker!!

Building success in thinking increases confidence. This increased confidence eventually leads to greater strength in reading – an important step toward *taking the numb out of numbers.*

THE NAME DROPPER

Weird name was teen's grad present

CARPINTERIA, Calif. (AP) – A teenager, casting about for a new name, has reeled in a golden one: *Trout Fishing in America.*

The 17-year-old wanted to do something different for his upcoming graduation from Carpinteria High School. So he went to court last week to legally change his name from Peter Eastman to *Trout Fishing in America.*

Trout said he decided to change his name to break away from tradition.

"I am just saying I am not this little kid anymore. I want to be my own person."

The name was inspired by Richard Brautigan's 1967 counterculture classic, Trout Fishing in America. "I really liked the book," Trout said. "He looks at the world in the way I like."

Peter Eastman Sr. said he supports his son's decision, but said he was sad that the family torch has been passed to a fish.

Still, the senior Eastman paid the $182 name-change filing fee as a graduation present for his son. It should become official in a couple of weeks and the name *Trout Fishing in America* should appear on his diploma in June.

MR. EASTMAN WHO WAS NOT ONLY GENEROUS, BUT FAIR, OFFERED TO CHANGE THE NAMES OF ALL HIS 5 CHILDREN, INCLUDING 'TROUT'- IF HE COULD DO IT FOR UNDER $1000.

IS THIS POSSIBLE? EXPLAIN.

TRY TO ANSWER THIS QUESTION WITHOUT PAPER AND PENCIL AND WITHOUT A CALCULATOR — IN OTHER WORDS USE MENTAL MATH!

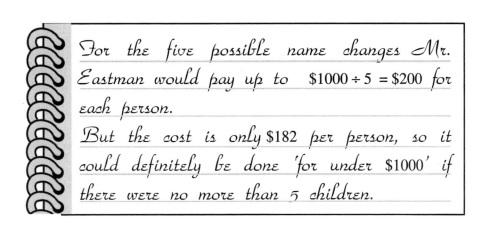

For the five possible name changes Mr. Eastman would pay up to $1000 ÷ 5 = $200 for each person.

But the cost is only $182 per person, so it could definitely be done 'for under $1000' if there were no more than 5 children.

STUDENTS HESITATED TO USE MENTAL MATH.

MANY FOUND $182 × 5 = $910 WITH PAPER AND PENCIL.

STILL OTHERS DID IT BY REPEATED ADDITION (WHICH IS WHAT MULTIPLICATION MEANS).

```
  182
  182
  182
  182
  182
  910
```

Once again simple mental math and thinking can replace more complicated paper and pencil work.

For many students reading is a problem. This includes those for whom English is a second language. A tape recorder is useful for minimizing reading without diminishing the problem solving. A good reader could read the clipping aloud and tape the reading. Then all can listen to the tape and answer the questions.

Another way to help weak readers is to have the students work in pairs. One student can read the clipping aloud, or the students can read alternate paragraphs, helping each other understand difficult words. Then both students can answer the question. An interesting newspaper clipping encourages all students to read!

WHAT'S THE DIFFERENCE?

SOME OF 'LAST NIGHT'S' BASKETBALL SCORES...

ATLANTA 107,   L.A. CLIPPERS 88
NEW YORK 101,   ORLANDO 86
TORONTO 112,   PHILADELPHIA 90
DETROIT 108,   CHICAGO 91
HOUSTON 113,   SEATTLE 73

FIND THE DIFFERENCE IN POINTS BETWEEN THE WINNING AND LOSING TEAMS IN 'LAST NIGHT'S' GAMES, WITHOUT USING A CALCULATOR OR PAPER AND PENCIL!

INTERNET

EXPLORATION

YOU CAN FIND THE LATEST NBA SCORES DIRECTLY FROM THE INTERNET AT THE ADDRESS BELOW.

SEE IF YOU CAN CALCULATE MENTALLY THE DIFFERENCES IN SOME OF LAST NIGHT'S SCORES.

VISIT THIS WEBSITE
http://www.nba.com

The differences are...

107 − 88 = 19

101 − 86 = 15

112 − 90 = 22

108 − 91 = 17

113 − 73 = 40

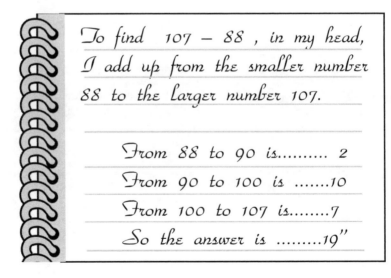

To find 107 − 88 , in my head, I add up from the smaller number 88 to the larger number 107.

From 88 to 90 is.......... 2
From 90 to 100 is 10
From 100 to 107 is........7
So the answer is ....19"

S ubtracting, by adding up from the smaller number to the larger number can be done mentally in many ways. For example, here are at least two more paths to finding 107 – 88.

From 88 to 98 is ...10
From 98 to 100 is ...2
From 100 to 107 is ..7
So the answer is 19

or

From 88 to 98 is ...10
From 98 to 108 is ..10
From 108 to 107 is −1
So the answer is 19

Finding different ways to arrive at the same answer increases a person's confidence in doing math which helps *take the numb out of numbers.*

Many people use this method of subtracting for making change in a store!

Sports provide a rich source of numbers and interest for many people. Doing math about things you care about also helps *take the numb out of numbers.*[*]

---

*For more sports math ideas for girls and boys see *Yesterday's Sports, To-Day's Math* , written by Don Fraser and published by Cuisenaire & Dale Seymour Publications.

You Be the Coach

Whether you're a basketball fan or not you still may be the best coach in your classroom! Choose a team that is popular with your students. For example if you live in Arizona you might choose the Phoenix Suns.

Have each student choose three players from your local team whom he or she thinks will score the most points **in their next game**. If you or they don't know three players – no problem! You can access the names of the players at **http://sports.yahoo.com/nba/teams**. On that page select the name of your team. Then, under the heading **Individual Leaders**, click on **complete team statistics**. A table will be displayed listing all the players in the first column and the average number of points per game (PPG) in the last column.

For example, the table displayed for the Phoenix Suns as of June 14, 2007 gave these points-per-game averages for the season.

Player	PPG
Stoudemire	20.4
Nash	18.6
Barbosa	18.1
Marion	17.5
Bell	14.7
Diaw	9.7
Jones	6.4
Banks	4.9
Thomas	4.6
Rose	3.7

Students list their top three predictions of the leading point scorers for the Sun's next game, but they leave the points spaces blank.

My Choices: Points

#1. _____   _____

#2. _____   _____

#3. _____   _____

Total   _____

Based on past data, students might be tempted to choose Stoudemire, Nash and Barbarosa. But in any particular game we don't know how each player will do. Have a student bring in the boxscore from the Suns' next game. Then each 'coach' should write in how many points his or her three players scored and the total. The best coach is the one who chose the three players with the most points.

This basketball activity is very versatile in that it can involve games and teams from elementary school right through to the pros – women and men!

A similar activity with baseball batting averages is also very popular! The activity is the same as basketball except we calculate the total batting average rather than the total points. We use the equation:

Combined Batting Average = Hits divided by *At Bats*

	My Choices:	Hits	At Bats
#1.	_____	_____	_____
#2.	_____	_____	_____
#3.	_____	_____	_____
	Total	_____	_____
Combined batting average = Hits ÷ At Bats =			

The student with the highest combined batting average is the winner!

To determine which of two batting averages is larger, students will sometimes compare common fractions. In other cases they may convert their fractions to decimals. Many students find this a motivational context for comparing fractions.

PREDICTING THE WINNER

Several of the previous activities have been embedded in a sports context, because every classroom has some students who are interested in athletics. Sports data are a rich source of information that students will find meaningful. In particular, baseball, basketball, hockey and football statistics for recent games are readily available in many newspapers and on the Internet (some URLs have been given in previous activities). Summaries (sometimes called "boxscores") give useful data on a particular game. For example, on April 29, 2006 an event occurred that happens about once every 20 years!

In a baseball game between the New York Yankees and the Toronto Blue Jays, the winning team, (the Yankees) scored in every inning that they came to bat. Part of the boxscore summarizing this game looked like this:

Inning	1	2	3	4	5	6	7	8	9	Score
Blue Jays	2	0	3	0	1	0	0	0	0	6
Yankees	4	1	2	2	3	1	3	1	X	17

The columns give the runs scored by each team in each inning and the last column gives the final score for each team. Use boxscores to give students an early introduction to statistical ideas by using these data to test hypotheses such as the following.

Baseball

The winning team (in a particular game) is...

- the team that scores first.

- the team that is winning at the end of the seventh inning.

- the team that scores the most runs in a single inning.

Formulating and testing hypotheses is also possible using boxscores from other sports such as those suggested below.

Basketball

The winning team (in a particular game) is...

- the team that is winning at half-time.

- the team with more offensive rebounds.

- the team with the higher assists to turnovers ratio.

- the team with the better shooting average.

Football

The winning team is ...

- the team that is winning at the end of the 3rd quarter.

- the team with the most yards gained rushing in that game.

The team with the quarterback who has the highest passing average.

Hockey

The winning team is ...

- the team that scores first.

- the team with the most shots-on-goal.

- the team with fewer penalties.

Encourage the students to create their own investigations using 'boxscores'!

REASONABLE

OR

UNREASONABLE?

Walnut Cove

IS THE ANSWER REASONABLE OR UNREASONABLE?

Marcia Clark's first words to the jury in the O . J. Simpson trial were…

"You must look at the evidence and decide…
Is this reasonable?
Is this logical?
Does this make sense?"

My daughter says, "Please lend me $20, but only give me $10. That way you'll owe me $10, and I'll owe you $10, and we'll be even."

IS THAT REASONABLE?

'Heading' soccer ball can lower IQ

By Marilyn Elias
USA TODAY

NEW YORK – Frequently "heading" the ball in soccer lowers players' IQs and impairs their ability to concentrate, suggests a new study.

Soccer is relatively safe for most players, says psychologist Adrienne Witol of Medical College of Virginia, Richmond, but those who head the ball 10 or more times a game are at risk for brain damage that lowers intellectual function. "It may be time to look at designing a protective helmet," she told the American Psychological Association over the weekend.

Witol tested 60 male soccer players ages 14-29 who played up to five times a week. Those who averaged 10 or more headers a game did significantly worse on mental concentration than non-players or those who head less often; their IQs averaged 103, vs. 112 for those heading once or less a game.

DO YOU AGREE?

CLOSE THE FRIDGE!

> On average, Americans open their refrigerators 22 times a day.
>
> – Harper's Index*

---

* Harper's magazine is an excellent source of fascinating statements. Examining their truth provides an entertaining way of *taking the numb out of numbers.*

IS THIS STATEMENT REASONABLE OR UNREASONABLE?

CONVINCE ME!

SEARCH THE INTERNET USING THE KEY WORDS: **HARPER'S INDEX**.

BROWSE SOME OF THE SITES YOU FIND INTERESTING. FIND A FACT OR FACTOID INVOLVING NUMBERS. THEN STATE WHETHER YOU THINK IT'S REASONABLE OR UNREASONABLE AND WHY.

There is no way that this is true even if you exaggerate. Let's say you open the refrigerator door 5 times at breakfast, 5 times at lunch, and 5 times at dinner. This would be 15 times a day.

It depends how many members are in the family. There are six members in my family so our refrigerators are opened six times more than those who live on their own.

I took a survey on this. 6 people said it was reasonable and 2 people said it was unreasonable. I think it's reasonable.

True! On average an American family has 4 people.
Kid #1 : Snack 2, Breakfast 1..
Kid #2: Snack 2, Breakfast 1
Mother: Breakfast 2, Lunch 2, Dinner 2, Dessert 2, Snack 2
Dad: Lunch, Breakfast, Lunch, Dinner, Dessert, Snack
Total...22 times
Resource: Cousin's house, Cleveland Ohio

I believe so because I went around my apartment building asking and watching how many times my neighbors opened their refrigerators. Added altogether it was 989 times and 18 people.
Average? 0.0182002

This last student has used a calculator but divided 18 by 989 instead of 989 by 18 – an easy mistake to make - even with a calculator! That's why it is important that students check to see if the final answer makes sense.

Remember: After you answer the question, then question the answer.

A number of years ago this investigation would not have been considered an appropriate exercise in mathematics! However, since the publication of *The Standards for Curriculum and Evaluation* by The National Council Of Teachers Of Mathematics (NCTM) in 1989, such investigations are encouraged as a basis for developing number sense. In 2000, the NCTM published a sequel to this document titled, *Principles and Standards for School Mathematics*. Among the ten standards enunciated in that document are the following five that identify the major components of a complete mathematics program.

1. Problem Solving
2. Reasoning and proof
3. Communication
4. Connections
5. Representation

These standards are explained in greater detail on pages 216-218. Observe how many of these standards come into play in this "refrigerator" activity .

Cookie Math

On average, a Canadian will eat 35,000 cookies in a lifetime.

IS THIS STATEMENT REASONABLE OR UNREASONABLE?

WHY?

HERE ARE SOME STUDENT ANSWERS:

"I think it's not only unreasonable, but freakin' impossible ..."

"Yes. It's so reasonable. I <u>know</u> (not think) that because there are 365 days in a year and you probably won't eat cookies every day. So let's say the average Canadian eats 300 cookies in a year. The average Canadian lives to about 75. So 300x75= 22,500 which is close to 35,000 (the real answer). I'm only 12,500 cookies off!"

"Different people eat different amounts of cookies per day. So for different people, they would get different cookie answers."

"I usually eat 5 cookies per week. In a month I eat 5x4 = 20 cookies. In a year I eat 12x20 = 240 cookies. If I eat cookies for 65 years, then I would eat 240x65= 15,600 cookies! It is reasonable for people who love cookies to eat 35,000 cookies in their lifetime. But for me 35,000 cookies is too much. The most I would take is 15,600 cookies in my life. Therefore it is unreasonable for me."

"I think that it is unreasonable. If the average Canadian eats that much in a lifetime, I can divide that number by 78 (the average life expectancy of an average Canadian) and then I'll know how much an average Canadian eats in one year. 35,000 divided by 78 = 449 (rounded). Now I can take that number and divide by 52 and I'll have the number of cookies an average Canadian will eat in a week. 449 divided by 52 = 8 (rounded). Then I can take that number and divide it by 7 (days in a week). 8 divided by 7 is a little more than 1. So an average Canadian eats **at least** 1 cookie a day. That's crazy! I don't eat 1 cookie a week!!. It's really unhealthy to eat so much sugar all the time. Imagine what would happen to your teeth!

Deciding if a statement of fact is reasonable or not is just one of the many ways to increase number sense and to link number sense to literacy.

The student answers that appear on the two preceding pages came from students in the classes of Chad Soon, a dedicated educator who teaches in a Toronto school. These responses reveal that the children in Mr. Soon's class have already learned how to use the four arithmetic operations to make estimates and to test the plausibility of various claims they may find in the media. This is a major step toward the acquisition of mathematical literacy.

Mr. Soon has many creative ideas that he is willing to share. You can contact him at: chadbsoon@hotmail.com

THEY PROBABLY HAVE ALLERGIES

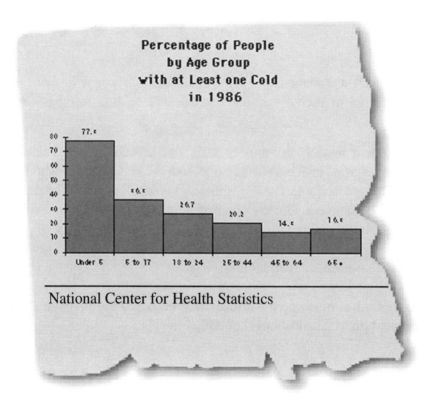

Percentage of People
by Age Group
with at Least one Cold
in 1986

National Center for Health Statistics

DOES THIS GRAPH SEEM REASONABLE OR UNREASONABLE ?

ARE YOU SURPRISED BY ANYTHING IN THE GRAPH?

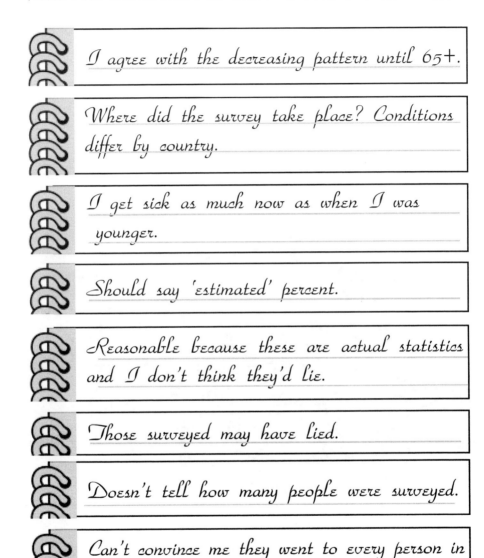

I agree with the decreasing pattern until 65+.

Where did the survey take place? Conditions differ by country.

I get sick as much now as when I was younger.

Should say 'estimated' percent.

Reasonable because these are actual statistics and I don't think they'd lie.

Those surveyed may have lied.

Doesn't tell how many people were surveyed.

Can't convince me they went to every person in the country. Besides I had a cold that year and I don't know how they found out.

People surveyed would have a different definition of cold.

Parents answering for kids under five.

Maybe people forgot they had colds.

I don't think anyone could have caught a cold more than 65 times, and if they did it probably means they have allergies.

From the last student response, we are reminded of the importance of labelling the axes on a graph!

In the past year, how many times have you drawn a graph that wasn't a school assignment? Probably not very often! On the other hand, how many times have you looked at a graph in a book, magazine, or newspaper and said, "That's reasonable", "That's unreasonable", or "That's surprising"? Probably quite often!

Reading and interpreting graphs is a very useful math skill. Deciding if something is reasonable or not is a very useful life skill.

Do You Agree or Disagree?

LOOK AT EACH STATEMENT. USE CHECK MARKS TO INDICATE WHETHER YOU THINK THAT THE PERCENT IS TOO LOW, ABOUT RIGHT, OR TOO HIGH.

		Too Low	About Right	Too High
❶.	When handed a pen and asked to try it out, 97% write their own names.	◯	◯	◯
❷.	A toaster is found in 80% of households.	◯	◯	◯
❸.	70% of people wear glasses or contact lenses.	◯	◯	◯
❹.	51% are afraid of snakes.	◯	◯	◯
❺.	50% of adults live within 50 miles of where they grew up.	◯	◯	◯
❻.	The favorite pizza topping is pepperoni at 43%.	◯	◯	◯
❼.	When a new telephone book arrives, 38% look up their name.	◯	◯	◯
❽.	18% of coffee consumed is 'decaf'.	◯	◯	◯
❾.	12% say chicken soup is the best cure for a cold.	◯	◯	◯
❿.	8% drink nine or ten 8-ounce glasses of water daily.	◯	◯	◯

FOR THE TWO SURVEYS ON THIS PAGE AND THE NEXT,
MATCH THE CORRECT PERCENT WITH THE CATEGORY.

Survey 1

What are the most popular hot dog toppings? (i.e., what percent of
people use each topping?)

Ketchup _____

Mustard _____

Onions _____

Relish _____

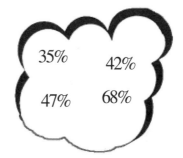

35%   42%

47%   68%

According to surveys con-
ducted by the media, each of
the statements given on the
previous page is true – but
that's only if you believe
everything you read!

For fascinating graphs and interesting facts, see:
www.usatoday.com/news/snapshot.htm

Survey 2

How many people do we usually have Thanksgiving dinner with?

5 or fewer _____

6 to 10 _____

11 to 15 _____

16 to 20 _____

21 or more _____

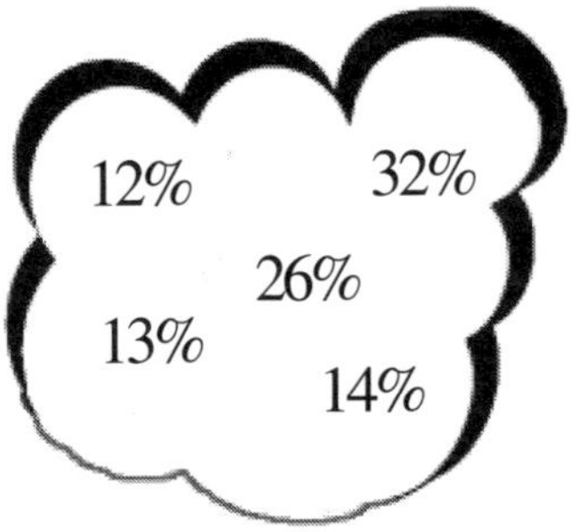

12%   32%
     26%
13%
        14%

SURVEY YOUR CLASS TO SEE
IF YOU GET RESULTS
SIMILAR TO YOURS.

W hen teaching reading, a standard technique is to pause at a certain point in the story and predict what will happen next. This increases interest in the story. We can apply this idea to teaching mathematics by having students predict the results of a survey before they conduct it.

Answers to survey #1: 47%, 68%, 42%, 35%.

Answers to survey #2: 13%, 32%, 26%, 12%, 14%.

Have the class conduct each of the two surveys and compare their results with those given in the answers.

M & M 's

40 % of M & M's are Brown

– USA TODAY

IS THIS A REASONABLE OR AN UNREASONABLE STATEMENT ?

WRITE A PARAGRAPH EXPLAINING WHY.

INTERNET

EXPLORATION

WOULD YOU BELIEVE THAT THERE IS AN M & M ON-LINE SOFTWARE CATALOG ON THE INTERNET?

EXPLORE SOME OF THE SOFTWARE AVAILABLE FOR ELEMENTARY MATHEMATICS.

VISIT THIS WEBSITE **http://www.mm-soft.com/**

FOR THIS INVESTIGATION EACH GROUP WAS GIVEN A PACKAGE OF M&M 'S.

HERE IS A SAMPLE OF EXPLANATIONS...

> 15/33   15 were brown and I got the % and got 45%

> Result of class... Brown 214   Total 562
> 214/562 = 38%

> To find out the answer I counted a package of M&M's and found out... 26% were brown, 25% were yellow, 21% were blue, 12% were red, 8% were orange, 8% were green. Therefore, I conclude that 40% are not brown.

> I think this is reasonable. A package of M&M's has five colors, brown, dark brown, yellow, green, and orange. If these colors equal 100% then each color shares 20%. To sum up, brown and dark brown equals 40%.

> I think it is unreasonable because every pack is different. But in my group's package 37% were brown. I don't think it is reasonable.

Reasonable because it's 36% and it's close to 40% and the people who put them in don't have time to count how many colors are in a package. They care about the gram.

First I counted all the M&M's, then I counted the Brown's. There were 5. So my cousin said it's 15% so I said, oh!

I think it is unreasonable because when I opened a bag there were more reds than any other color.

I think it is reasonable because it doesn't matter what color it is. They all taste the same!

C onnecting math to the students' world, as with the M&M's, increases motivation. We observe that one student answered "40% are not brown", when she meant to indicate that the brown M& M's do not constitute 40% of the total. Language and math go together!

How Well Do You Know America?

Alaska

Hawaii

MATCH THE PERCENTS WITH THE CORRECT CATEGORY

WHAT PERCENT OF AMERICANS...

COUNT PACKAGES OF THE PERSON
IN FRONT OF THEM IN AN EXPRESS
CHECK-OUT LINE? _____
(SEE P. 33.)

EAT A SALAD DAILY? _____

HAVE BOUGHT STATE LOTTO
TICKETS IN THE PAST YEAR?
_____

HAVE SHOWERED WITH A PET?
(SEE P. 32.) _____

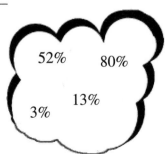

52%   80%

13%

3%

ALL ABOUT YOU!

TAKING SURVEYS? HERE ARE SOME INTERESTING THINGS TO FIND OUT ABOUT YOUR FRIENDS.

FIRST, CHECK OUT YOURSELF!

1. ARE YOU LEFT- OR RIGHT-THUMBED? _____

(CLASP YOUR HANDS BY INTERLOCKING YOUR FINGERS. IF YOUR LEFT THUMB IS OVER YOUR RIGHT THUMB, THEN YOU ARE LEFT-THUMBED. OTHERWISE YOU ARE RIGHT-THUMBED.)

2. ARE YOU A LEFT- OR A RIGHT-CLAPPER? _____

(CLAP YOUR HANDS. IF YOUR LEFT HAND IS OVER YOUR RIGHT HAND, THEN YOU ARE A LEFT-CLAPPER. OTHERWISE YOU ARE A RIGHT-CLAPPER.)

3. ARE YOU LEFT- OR RIGHT-LEGGED? _____

(CROSS YOUR LEGS. IF YOUR LEFT LEG IS OVER YOUR RIGHT LEG THEN YOU ARE LEFT-LEGGED. OTHERWISE YOU ARE RIGHT-LEGGED.)

4. ARE YOU A LEFT- OR A RIGHT-LICKER? _____

(PRETEND YOU ARE LICKING AN ENVELOPE. IF YOU LICK FROM LEFT TO RIGHT, THEN YOU ARE A LEFT-LICKER. OTHERWISE YOU ARE A RIGHT-LICKER.)

5. ARE YOU A LEFT- OR A RIGHT-GRIPPER? _____

(FOLD YOUR ARMS ACROSS YOUR CHEST. IF YOUR LEFT HAND IS GRIPPING YOUR RIGHT BICEP, THEN YOU ARE A LEFT-GRIPPER. OTHERWISE YOU ARE A RIGHT-GRIPPER.)

ALL ABOUT YOU! (CONT'D)

COLLECT DATA FROM YOUR FRIENDS AND USE A TALLY TO FILL IN THE CHART:

	Left	Right
Thumbed		
Clapper		
Legged		
Licker		
Gripper		

FROM THE CHART WHAT CONCLUSIONS CAN YOU DRAW?

DID YOU KNOW THAT, ACCORDING TO RESEARCH, TWO OUT OF THREE HUMANS ARE RIGHT-KISSERS? THIS MEANS THAT MOST HUMANS WHEN THEY ARE KISSING ON THE LIPS TILT THEIR HEAD TO THE RIGHT. CHECK IT OUT!

AS EASY AS 1, 2, 3 ...

HERE'S A TRICK TO AMAZE YOUR FRIENDS AND FAMILY!

WRITE DOWN THE NUMBERS: 1, 2, 3, 4

WITHOUT THINKING, CIRCLE ONE OF THE FOUR NUMBERS.

DID YOU KNOW THAT IN A GROUP OF 20 OR MORE, MOST PEOPLE WILL CIRCLE 3 ?

WHY? IT'S A MYSTERY!

MOST STUDENTS INSIST ON THINKING.

HERE ARE SOME OF THE REASONS THEY HAVE GIVEN FOR THEIR CHOICES:

> I chose #1 because I didn't want to be the same as my other classmates and I thought they would choose #3 or #4. I was right!
>
> I chose #1 because that number is rich people's choice cause they always want to be first.
>
> I chose #2 because I closed my eyes and landed on #2.

I chose #2 because the month of my birthday is the 2nd month and the day is two 2's. My birthday is February 22.

I chose #2 because my little sister is 2 years old.

I chose #3 because 3 is the first number that comes to my head when I hear the word **number**.

I like #3 because it's kind of in the middle.

I chose #3 because when I was 3 years old I could talk.

I chose #4 because I just like drawing that number when we have free time.

I chose #4 because that's how many Lego guys I have.

I chose #4 because it was the highest of them all.

I chose #4 because that was when my brother was most annoying.

I chose #4 because at four I came to school had fun and made friends. It was the best time of my life.

I chose #4 because that was when I got my ears pierced.

In most of these experiments #4 was chosen much more then #1 and #2, but not as much as #3!

Ask your students what they think will be the most frequently chosen number if the numbers 2, 3, 4, 5 are displayed. Conduct a survey within the class to check whether the majority of students were correct in their conjecture.

Invite your students to think of other experiments that they might try. After conducting a class survey, ask students to conjecture about the outcomes of the survey. Then have them compare their conjectures with the actual data. This process not only heightens the interest in the survey results, but it also helps students understand the process of testing conjectures.

By conducting surveys of several classes, students learn that the results of a survey often change as the sample size is increased, but usually stabilize as the sample size becomes very large. From this, the student learns to mistrust conclusions based on small samples.

INDUCTIVE

&

SEDUCTIVE

REASONING

From early childhood, we observe that the sun rises every morning. We therefore expect that the sun will rise tomorrow morning. This form of reasoning in which we generalize from past experience is called *inductive reasoning*.

In mathematics, we might search for patterns in lists of numbers and use this pattern to guess the next term in the list. But how many numbers or examples are needed before we can generalize? In mathematics, as in life, generalizing from only a few examples does not always lead to a valid conclusion. Beware of jumping to conclusions too soon.

Births
Doctors Hospital

Parents and gender of child
Melanie & Fred Koplin, girl
Maria and Paulo Hernandez, girl

Conclusion: Doctors Hospital gives birth to girls only!

Mind Over Basketball

Ten volunteers who had never played basketball scored an average of 3 free throws every 20 attempts.

Five days later, after practicing only in their minds, they averaged 5 free throws every 20 attempts.

Conclusion: Mental visualization improves performance.

Women's Tennis

Hingis defeated Vicario	6-2, 6-2
Coetzer defeated Graf	6-1, 6-4
Majoli defeated Dragomir	6-3, 5-7, 6-2

Conclusion: If you win the first set, you'll win the match.

Women's Golf

Four LPGA Tournament Winners

Betsy King	71-67-67-71	– 276
Donna Andrews	68-67-70-68	– 273
Annika Sorenstam	73-68-71-73	– 285
Laura Davies	70-69-70-68	– 277

Conclusion: The winner always does better in the second round than in the first round.

ARE YOU STREET SMART?

THE TOP TEN OF EVERYTHING, A BOOK BY RUSSELL ASH LISTS THE TEN MOST POPULAR STREET NAMES IN AMERICA. ACCORDING TO THE BOOK, FOURTH STREET IS RANKED #4 AND FIFTH STREET IS RANKED #5!

RANK	NAME
#1	_____
#2	_____
#3	_____
#4	FOURTH STREET
#5	FIFTH STREET

AS IT TURNS OUT THE TOP 10 ARE....

RANK	STREET NAME
#1	SECOND STREET
#2	PARK STREET
#3	THIRD STREET
#4	FOURTH STREET
#5	FIFTH STREET
#6	FIRST STREET
#7	SIXTH STREET
#8	SEVENTH STREET
#9	WASHINGTON STREET
#10	MAPLE STREET

Most people hesitate to use inductive reasoning with just two examples. They are skeptical that the pattern continues yet they feel that because it is math, there must be a pattern. For those who break the pattern, Main Street is a popular answer. According to the book, most towns and cities do not have a Main Street *and* a First Street so that neither was number one.

There are many topics in mathematics that offer students opportunities to explore patterns and apply inductive reasoning to formulate and test conjectures.

One student looked at the two subtractions shown below and conjectured that he could change every subtraction question into a multiplication question to obtain the correct answer!

$$\frac{1}{2} - \frac{1}{3} = \frac{3}{6} - \frac{2}{6} = \frac{1}{6}$$
$$\frac{1}{2} \times \frac{1}{3} = \frac{1 \times 1}{2 \times 3} = \frac{1}{6}$$

$$\frac{1}{5} - \frac{1}{6} = \frac{6}{30} - \frac{5}{30} = \frac{1}{30}$$
$$\frac{1}{5} \times \frac{1}{6} = \frac{1 \times 1}{5 \times 6} = \frac{1}{30}$$

Look at this seductive way to add two fractions.

$$\frac{2}{7} + \frac{3}{7} = \frac{23 + 32}{77} = \frac{55}{77} = \frac{5}{7}$$

$$\frac{2}{9} + \frac{5}{9} = \frac{25 + 52}{99} = \frac{77}{99} = \frac{7}{9}$$

You can see why this section is titled 'inductive & seductive reasoning'.

SUDOKU 数独

SUDOKU (MEANING "SINGLE NUMBER") IS A PUZZLE THAT BECAME POPULAR IN JAPAN IN 1986.

TRY SOLVING THE SUDOKU PUZZLE BELOW BY FOLLOWING THIS INSTRUCTION:

USE THE DIGITS 1,2,3,4 TO COMPLETE THIS PUZZLE SO THAT ALL FOUR DIGITS ARE IN EACH ROW AND IN EACH COLUMN, AS WELL AS IN EACH 2 X 2 SQUARE.

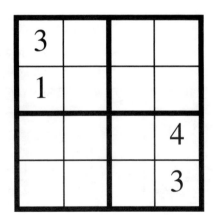

CAN YOU FIND MORE THAN ONE SOLUTION TO THIS SUDOKU PUZZLE?

A SUDOKU PUZZLE CAN BE MANY SIZES.

COMPLETE THIS SUDOKU BY FILLING IN THE MISSING NUMBER. ENSURE THAT ALL THE DIGITS FROM 1 TO 9 APPEAR EXACTLY ONCE IN EACH ROW COLUMN AND 3 X 3 SQUARE.

	3	1	9	7	8	2	5	6
2	6	9	1	3	5	7	4	8
8	7	5	2	6	4	9	3	1
7	5	4	3	8	6	1	9	2
6	8	2	4	1	9	5	7	3
9	1	3	5	2	7	8	6	4
5	2	8	7	4	3	6	1	9
1	4	7	6	9	2	3	8	5
3	9	6	8	5	1	4	2	7

IS THAT SUDUKO PUZZLE TOO EASY? TRY THIS ONE?

5	4	7	2	9	8	6	1	3
2	3	9	1	5	6	8	7	4
6	8	1	7	3	4	9	2	5
4	2	8				7	3	1
9	1	3				2	5	6
7	5	6				4	9	8
8	7	5	6	2	1	3	4	9
3	6	4	9	7	5	1	8	2
1	9	2	8	4	3	5	6	7

SUDOKU (CONT'D)

SUDOKU PUZZLES ARE NOW PUBLISHED IN BOOKS AND NEWSPAPERS AROUND THE WORLD.

HERE IS A SUDOKU PUZZLE.

4	9			2		1		
					6		4	
8		6	7		9	3		
9	6	8		3				1
			6	5	8			
5				1		8	2	6
		4	2		5	9		7
	7		3					
		9		7			3	4

THERE IS ONE SOLUTION TO THIS PUZZLE SO THAT EVERY ROW AND EVERY COLUMN USES ALL THE DIGITS 1 THROUGH 9.

ALSO EACH OF THE NINE MARKED 3X3 GRIDS ALSO USE ALL THE DIGITS 1 THROUGH 9. TO HELP YOU GET STARTED SEE WWW.SUDOKU.COM

The correct answer to this Sudoku puzzle is given below. Note that the arithmetic properties of the numbers are irrelevant. Any set of nine distinct symbols could be used instead of the numerals. Sudoku puzzles help children practice trial-and-error approaches to problem solving. Trial-and-error is an important part of inductive reasoning.

4	9	7	5	2	3	1	6	8
2	3	5	1	8	6	7	4	9
8	1	6	7	4	9	3	5	2
9	6	8	4	3	2	5	7	1
7	2	1	6	5	8	4	9	3
5	4	3	9	1	7	8	2	6
3	8	4	2	6	5	9	1	7
1	7	2	3	9	4	6	8	5
6	5	9	8	7	1	2	3	4

Two websites www.sudoku.com and www.websudoku.com provide billions of puzzles as well as strategies and tips for solving them.

GOTCHA!

4,   12,   28,   ☐   , ...

WHAT IS THE NEXT TERM IN THIS SEQUENCE? WHY?

WHEN TEACHERS ATTENDING A WORKSHOP WERE PRE-
SENTED WITH THIS QUESTION, THEY PRODUCED SEV-
ERAL DIFFERENT ANSWERS.

THE MOST POPULAR ANSWER WAS 52.

ONE REASON GIVEN FOR 52 IS BASED ON A
PATTERN OF DIFFERENCES:

From 4 to 12 is 8,
from 12 to 28 is 16,
from 28 to 52 is 24.

ANOTHER PATTERN WHICH LED TO THE ANSWER 52
IS "THE SQUARES OF ODD NUMBERS, PLUS 3."

Odd numbers	1	3	5	7
Squares	1	9	25	49
Squares +3	4	12	28	52

ANOTHER PATTERN YIELDED THE ANSWER 60.

THIS CAN BE SHOWN THROUGH A PATTERN OF
DIFFERENCES:

From 4 to 12 is 8,
From 12 to 28 is 16,
From 28 to 60 is 32.

Of course there is no one 'right' answer. *To take the numb out of numbers,* students are encouraged to look for patterns and to look for different answers to a problem and also to look for different approaches to arrive at the same answer. All this happened when this problem was used with the students in a variety of classrooms.

Reflecting on his own scientific discoveries, Nobel prizewinner John Polyani observed,

> *Inherited curiosity led me to study different approaches to finding the ... solution to a problem or question.*

Actually the answer I was thinking of was not 52 or 60, but 31. Why? It was the next number in a set of winning lottery numbers!

4 12 28 31 45 46, bonus 6
Record jackpot gets even bigger –$26.2 million

GOTCHA!!

THE PROBLEM WITH WORD PROBLEMS IS WORDS

Cats Take a Licking

Most adult cats spend 18 hours a day napping. Half their waking hours are spent licking themselves, according to *Kittens USA* magazine.

DOES THIS MEAN THEY SPEND 3 HOURS A DAY LICKING THEMSELVES?

Boy mayor's new broom sweeping Texas town clean

CRABB, Texas (UPI) – An 11-year-old boy who is unofficially the youngest mayor ever elected in the United States says his main goal is to incorporate his community of 75 people into a town.

Then his status will be official.

Mayor Brian Zimmerman – in office since October when he received 23 of 30 votes cast at Gonya's Grocery store – has brought about the grading of the dusty main street, mulled over whether to pave it and participated as pitcher and shortstop on the town baseball team.

"I was interested in being mayor because the work around here needed to be done," Brian said.

IS IT TRUE THAT FEWER THAN HALF THE PEOPLE IN THE TOWN VOTED FOR BRIAN ZIMMERMAN?

The Ten Percent Town

The telephone company announced today that 10% of all the people in this town have unlisted numbers.

IF YOU CHOSE 100 NAMES AT RANDOM FROM THE TOWN'S PHONE BOOK, ABOUT HOW MANY OF THOSE SELECTED WOULD HAVE UNLISTED NUMBERS?

WHY IS THE ANSWER 0 NOT 10?

A Most Valuable Player

USE ARITHMETIC AND COMMON SENSE TO HELP YOU FILL IN THE BLANKS BELOW

DID YOU KNOW THAT ALEX RODRIQUEZ MADE $25,680,732 WHILE PLAYING FOR THE NEW YORK YANKEES IN 2006?

HE PLAYED IN 154 REGULAR SEASON GAMES, WHICH MEANS, ON AVERAGE, HE EARNED _____ FOR EACH GAME.

ASSUMING EACH GAME WAS 9 INNINGS,

HE MADE _____ PER INNING.

IN 2006, RODRIQUEZ HAD 166 HITS .

HIS PAY WAS _____ FOR EACH HIT!

SURF THE INTERNET USING SEARCH WORDS LIKE **SALARIES** AND **INCOME**. RECORD SOME OF THE SALARIES YOU FIND.

ARE MOST ARTICLES ABOUT LARGE SALARIES OR SMALL SALARIES? WHY DO YOU THINK THIS IS SO?

TALK ABOUT IT...

IF YOU RAN THE ECONOMIC SYSTEM, WHAT JOBS DO
YOU FEEL WOULD BE WORTH THIS TYPE OF MONEY?

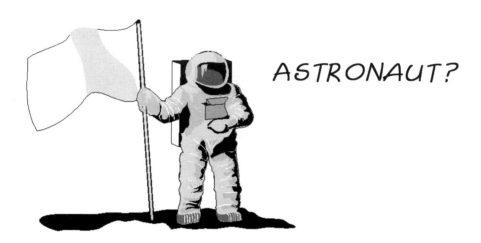

ASTRONAUT?

ATHLETE?

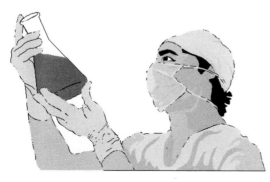

RESEARCH
SCIENTIST?

THE ANSWERS (TO THE NEAREST DOLLAR) ARE:

$25,680,732 ÷ 154 = $166,758.
$166,758 ÷ 9 = $18,529.
$25,680 732 ÷ 166 = $154,703.

ONE STUDENT WROTE:

> *I don't think any of the T.V., movie, and sports stars deserve this type of money. A scientist, doctor, a policeperson doing dangerous work and only the very best math teachers deserve this type of money!*

NEEDLESS TO SAY, THE STUDENT WHO WROTE THIS EARNED AN 'A' IN MATH THAT TERM.

To solve this problem, students must read and understand the clipping, select the numbers that are needed to solve the problem, then select the correct arithmetic operation. Finally, they have to do accurate arithmetic.

Years ago the following tongue-in-cheek rules for solving word problems were printed...

RULE 1. IF AT ALL POSSIBLE, AVOID READING THE PROBLEM. READING THE PROBLEM ONLY CONSUMES TIME AND CAUSES CONFUSION.

RULE 2. EXTRACT THE NUMBERS FROM THE PROBLEM IN THE ORDER IN WHICH THEY APPEAR. BE ON THE WATCH FOR NUMBERS WRITTEN IN WORDS.

RULE 3. IF RULE 2 YIELDS THREE OR MORE NUMBERS, THE BEST BET FOR GETTING THE ANSWER IS ADDING THEM TOGETHER.

RULE 4. IF THERE ARE ONLY TWO NUMBERS WHICH ARE ABOUT THE SAME SIZE, THEN SUBTRACTION SHOULD GIVE THE BEST RESULTS.

RULE 5. IF THERE ARE ONLY TWO NUMBERS IN THE PROBLEM AND ONE IS MUCH SMALLER THAN THE OTHER, THEN DIVIDE IF IT GOES EVENLY – OTHERWISE MULTIPLY.

The sad part is that these rules often did work. *Taking the Numb out of Numbers* demands much more!

THE HORSE-TRADER

Woman Trades Horse For New Car

LANGLEY, B.C. (CP) – Barb Roccamatis offered an unusual trade-in on a new car – her 2½-year-old palomino gelding.

And the gelding, Cruzen, earned her an $1,800 trade-in on a $15,000 black 1992 Nissan NX sports coupe.

Roccamatis, a bank teller, picks up her car Sunday, her 19th birthday.

"It was a very unusual trade-in", admitted Bernie Rosenblatt, owner of King George Nissan.

Roccamatis knew she wouldn't get much for her old truck so she reluctantly put Cruzen up for sale.

"It was a really hard decision", she said yesterday.

Stabling costs are $200 a month. She said, "I couldn't afford to keep Cruzen and I really need a new car."

The horse will be boarded in the stables of one of the salesmen until it can be sold, probably next spring.

USING THE INFORMATION IN THE STORY...

❶. WRITE A WORD PROBLEM THAT HAS THE ANSWER $13,200.

❷. WRITE A DIFFERENT WORD PROBLEM THAT HAS THE ANSWER $2,400.

SOME WORD PROBLEMS MIGHT BE:

- HOW MUCH MONEY DOES ROCCAMATIS STILL OWE THE CAR DEALER?

- HOW MUCH WOULD IT COST TO KEEP THE HORSE IN A STABLE FOR ONE YEAR?

TALK ABOUT IT.

DO YOU HAVE A PET? IF SO, WOULD YOU 'TRADE YOUR PET IN' FOR SOMETHING ELSE?

GETTING ENGAGED

You know those word problems in math? About the train going through a tunnel at 200 miles per hour? I'd picture it happening at dawn and the smoke from the engine would be trailing behind it...

– movie star, Kevin Costner

Costner was a good problem solver in school because he used his imagination to picture what was going on in the story. He was ENGAGED in the problem!

One of the best techniques to get students engaged in the problem solving process is to have them make up questions to go with the story.

One such story is this:

> Samantha worked at a tree ornament factory during the holidays. She packed 59-cent ornaments in boxes. Nine of these ornaments could be packed in one box. Yesterday she packed 1125 of the 59-cent ornaments.

Make up a word problem which could be solved from information in the story.

The students don't have to use all the numbers in the story and may add some more of their own, e.g., hours worked, taxes etc.

Some teachers collect the questions generated by their students. Then each day, for a week, they give out the same story, but with a different question. That way the weaker readers get the repetition they need to learn vocabulary and everybody gets to think about a different problem.

Variety can sometimes be added to simple word problems by putting them in a game show format like Jeopardy! Not only is such variety the 'spice of life', but it is also invaluable insurance against the risk of boredom.

Finding a question to go with an answer makes the problem more difficult to solve, but it adds a challenge for stronger students.

This technique also encourages students to use their imagination and become engaged in the problem as described by Kevin Costner!

THE GOOD NEWS IS....

BANKOK (Reuter) - Hotel cashier Thanes Narkphong ,____, has got some good news and some bad news about his jail sentence according to a report by the Thai news agency.

The good news was that his prison sentence for embezzling about $ _____ was cut yesterday by an appeals court.

The bad news was that the _____ year jail sentence was reduced to 576 years.

The sentence was reduced _____ years on the grounds that his testimony had proven useful, the agency said.

IN THE NEWS ARTICLE THERE ARE FOUR BLANKS TO BE FILLED   HERE ARE SIX NUMBERS IN A CLOUD FROM WHICH TO CHOOSE FOUR NUMBERS TO FILL THE BLANKS

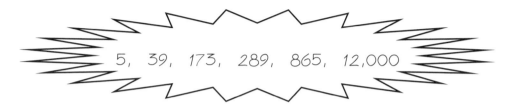

5, 39, 173, 289, 865, 12,000

USE LOGIC, COMMON SENSE, AND ARITHMETIC TO HELP YOU PUT THE NUMBERS IN THEIR CORRECT PLACE IN THE STORY.

THE ANSWERS, IN ORDER, IN THE STORY ARE 39, 12000, 865, AND 289. WHY?

 It seems reasonable that a cashier would be 39 years old.

 "...embezzling about..." implies a 'rounded' number like 12,000

 *Since the jail sentence was "reduced to 576 years" then the original sentence must have been more than 576 years. Therefore, the original sentence must have been 865 years.*

 Arithmetic confirms that 865 – 576 = 289

 *The numbers 5 and 173 do not make sense in this story.*

Notice that almost any newspaper clipping could be modified to fit this format! Having the students explain the reasons for their choices of numbers is a form of teaching. According to the National Teaching Laboratories in Bethel, Maine:

We retain 5% of what we hear at a lecture, 10% of what we read, 50% of what we discuss with others, and 90% of what we teach others.

AMERICAN IDOL

HERE IS A TABLE WITH THE NAMES, AGES, AND HOMETOWNS OF THE TWELVE AMERICAN IDOL FINALISTS IN 2007:

American Idol Finalists in 2007					
Men			Women		
Name	Age	Hometown	Name	Age	Hometown
Blake Lewis	23	Bothel, WA	Melinda Doolittle	29	Brentwood, TN
Sanjaya Malakar	17	Federal Way, WA	Stephanie Edwards	19	Savannah, GA
Chris Richardson	22	Chesapeake, VA	Gloria Glocksen	22	Naperville, IL
Brandon Rogers	28	North Hollywood, CA	Lakisha Jones	27	Fort Meade, MD
Chris Sligh	28	Greenville, SC	Haley Scarnato	24	San Antonio, TX
Phil Stacey	29	Jacksonville, FL	Jordin Sparks	17	Glendale, AZ

USING THIS DATA, YOU CAN MAKE LOTS OF WORD PROBLEMS LIKE THESE:

1. HOW OLD WILL MELINDA DOLITTLE BE WHEN JORDIN SPARKS IS 29 YEARS OLD?

2. HOW OLD WAS SANJAYA MALAKAR WHEN LAKISHA JONES WAS 19 YEARS OLD?

CREATE TWO WORD PROBLEMS AND SEE IF YOUR FRIENDS CAN SOLVE THEM.

150

American Idol contestants are sometimes asked to complete this sentence: "An American Idol is someone who ...."

One aspiring contestant wrote: "An American Idol is some who can inspire others to accomplish anything they set their mind to." This is what the best teachers do!

Word problems such as.... How old is Blake Lewis? How much older is Blake then Jordin? Find two contestants whose ages add to 50 .... are fine. However a more interesting question is...Who is older, the men or the women? Find two ways to justify your answer. This answer can change from week to week as contestants are eliminated.

Some teachers are very good at taking material from a contex that interests many students and using it to generate interest. One such teacher is Julia Bynum, from Asheville, NC who has created activities using shows such as *Survivor*, *The Amazing Race*, and *American Idol* to motivate her students. In an e-mail I received from Julia, she states,

I have made a wall for American Idol on the 8th grade hall. I put up a USA map with the American Idol logo above it. I printed out a brief bio of the 12 finalists with a picture of each. Then I placed them around the map with a piece of yarn stretching from the bio to where they live in the USA. To the side I have Idol math questions of the day. e.g., "What is the ratio of males to females of the remaining Idols?", "What percent of the Idols are from east of the Mississippi?" The kids can put their responses each day in my container and I draw a name from all correct responses for a prize the next day. The kids are excited so far!

I'm sure JB is the Teacher Idol of many of her students!

SPENDING SPREE

Teen goes on spending spree with $74,000 of parents' cash

OCEAN CITY, Md. (AP) – A teenager who got a bad report card took $74,000 from his parents, ran away to this seaside resort and went on a spending spree at $800-a-day, police said.

The 15-year-old runaway had $50,000 left when he was apprehended on the week-end at a go-cart track in West Ocean City, police said yesterday.

The boy left his suburban Pittsburgh home with $74,000 in a cardboard box, State Police Cpl. Harry Edwards said. His father was described as a self-employed businessman who often kept cash at home.

The teenager then hopped a bus to Ocean City and checked into a motel where rooms cost $32 to $34 a night.

He quickly made a friend, and together they rented a limousine for two days from Resort Transportation Co. A clerk said the boys had the driver take them shopping.

The boys ate mostly in pizza joints, "and everywhere they went, they tipped well", Edwards said.

The spree came to an end after the boy's parents learned of his whereabouts and contacted police. Police also were alerted by someone who found the teenager's spending habits unusual.

The boy was released to his mother Sunday afternoon.

DO YOU HAVE $74, OOO CASH IN A CARDBOARD BOX AT HOME?

IF THE ANSWER IS 'YES', PLEASE WRITE YOUR ADDRESS ON THIS PAGE. (HA HA!)

A. HOW MUCH MONEY DID THE BOY TAKE?

B. HOW MUCH DID HE HAVE LEFT?

C. HOW MUCH DID HE SPEND?

D. HOW MUCH DID HE SPEND EACH DAY?

E. HOW MANY DAYS DID HIS SPENDING SPREE LAST?

TALK ABOUT IT...

HOW WOULD YOU HAVE HANDLED A "BAD REPORT CARD"?

THE ANSWERS TO THE QUESTIONS ON THE PREVIOUS
PAGE ARE:

A. $74,000   B. $50,000

C. $74,000 – $50,000 = $24,000

D. $800   E. $24,000 ÷ $800 = 30 ; 30 DAYS

Question E, "How many days did his spending spree last?" is really a multi-step problem. When the problem is broken down into questions A,B,C,D, before question E is asked, much less thinking is required by the students.

However, students must learn to break down multi-step problems themselves. Helpful strategies include explaining the story to another person and acting out the story using smaller numbers. 'Guess and check' is also a useful strategy for students to see how the problem breaks down.

The story presented in the article is about 'money'. The final answer is in 'days'. The key is to link 'money' and 'days' with the "$800 - a- day" spending fact.

Solving word problems has been compared to crossing a small stream. Some can leap across the stream on their own, while others need some stepping stones, and still others need a bridge. The art of teaching is to provide the stepping stones and bridges where needed, but to encourage leaping across where possible!

TIEING THE KNOT

■ Marriage Licenses

(Tulsans unless otherwise noted)
Irma Steenberg, 19; Timothy Simmons, 19.
Ann Kao, 30; Dan Wu , 40, of Fort Worth.
Rebecca Graham, 27; Darryl Taylor, 28.
Kelli Carmel, 20; Michael Walker, 25.
Patricia Deevers, 17; Daniel Elliot Jr., 19,
both of Skiatook.
Jane Hedges, 27; David Catarino, 29.
Betty Wilson, 38; Stan Green, 49.
Donna Gibson, 42; Richard Danby, 40.
Carol Marley, 20; Kenneth Ainsley Jr., 24.
Jill Walker, 23; Brian Kilmer, 25.
Peggy Andersen, 32; Steven Kelly, 42.
Sharon Whetstone, 34; Benjamin Lam, 59.
Lisa Britnell, 27; Partick Donovan, 27.
Kimberly Janzen, 23; Travis Levy, 18, both of
Hominy
Brenda Nesbitt, 23; James Newton Jr., 33,
both of Broken Arrow.
Katherine Johnson, 27; Jack McBride Jr., 29
Denise Pettit 32; Charles Jenkins, 29.
Sherry Moore, 32; James Seibezzi, 36.
Michelle Laughton, 19; Phillip Jones, 19, both
of Owasso.
Liza Yamamoto, 33; Robert Trombetta, 30.
Amy Kepler, 18; Christopher Goldstein, 19.

❶. LOOK AT THIS DATA WHICH GIVES THE AGE OF EACH PERSON GETTING MARRIED.

IN A SMALL GROUP, SHARE IDEAS ABOUT WHAT EACH OF YOU FINDS INTERESTING AND WHAT YOU HAVE QUESTIONS ABOUT.

❷. USING INFORMATION FROM THE CLIPPING, MAKE UP A MATH QUESTION.

❸. WRITE UP A SOLUTION TO THE QUESTION YOU ASKED.

❹. TRADE QUESTIONS WITH A FRIEND. ANSWER EACH OTHER'S QUESTION.

❶. DURING SMALL GROUP DISCUSSIONS COMMENTS WERE HEARD, SUCH AS …

"Some of them got married so young."

"They got married at all ages."

"Why did Sharon Whetstone marry Benjamin Lam who is so much older than her? I don't know."

"Irma and Timothy are too young to get married."

"Most of the men are older than the women."

❷. STUDENTS CREATED A WIDE VARIETY OF MATH PROBLEMS. A SAMPLE OF THESE IS GIVEN HERE.

"How much older is Benjamin than Sharon?"

"Who is usually older, the man or the woman?"

"What is the average age of the women? The men?"

"Are most people who are getting married under or over 30 years old?"

When students determine some of the questions, they feel an ownership that is usually lacking in math. By trading questions, students are enriched by others' experiences – another step to *taking the numb out of numbers.*

As we observe students participating actively in their mathematical explorations, we are reminded of the oft-quoted Chinese proverb:

I HEAR AND I FORGET
I SEE AND I REMEMBER
I DO AND I UNDERSTAND

THINK, TALK, AND WRITE ABOUT IT!

THE NEWSPAPER HAS LOTS OF INTERESTING ARTICLES THAT ARE FUN TO THINK AND TALK ABOUT. HERE ARE FOUR EXAMPLES OF REAL ARTICLES.

❶

British businessman Tom Granby found he'd dived off the high board after he agreed to sponsor a charity swim by a young girl at a rate of $6 for every length of the pool she completed.

He expected to pay out maybe $100. But he didn't know that the girl was a marathon swimmer. She swam 1,214 lengths – and now Granby has received a reminder that his pledge works out to be over $7,000.

He's refusing to pay. London newspaper columnist, John Junior says: " I back him in that refusal. There are times when charity demands come perilously close to moral blackmail. And this is one of them."

1. EXACTLY HOW MUCH DOES GRANBY OWE?

2. HOW MANY METRES DID THE YOUNG GIRL SWIM?

THINK, TALK, & WRITE ABOUT IT

DO YOU THINK HE SHOULD HAVE TO PAY?

EXPLAIN YOUR REASONING?

160

❷

The Kozy Korner restaurant recently gave a cheque for $1,050 to the Haliburton Highlands Health Services Foundation. They reached this total over the last two years by pledging 25 cents for each cup of coffee sold.

HOW MANY CUPS OF COFFEE HAVE BEEN SOLD AT THE KOZY KORNER OVER THE LAST TWO YEARS?

THINK, TALK, & WRITE ABOUT IT

DO YOU THINK THE KOZY KORNER IS A SMALL OR LARGE RESTAURANT? WHY?

❸

Bill Dunlop, of Toronto, and Traci Dunlop, of Calgary, are among the four Canadians who have changed their last names to Dunlop-Tire. The four took the new names as part of the Dunlop Tired Of Your Name Challenge which dared about 1000 people with the last name Dunlop to legally change their names. The first 50 to do so were eligible to share $25,000 cash.

Their are no restrictions on how long the four have to keep their new names. Dunlop Tires had a survey done last year of 2000 Canadians. Thirty-seven percent said they would change their name for the right price, and 42 percent said they believed changing your name to adopt a corporate brand will become a new form of advertising.

HOW MUCH MONEY DID TRACI DUNLOP MAKE WHEN SHE CHANGED HER NAME TO TRACI DUNLOP-TIRE?

THINK, TALK, & WRITE ABOUT IT

WOULD YOU CHANGE YOUR NAME TO THE NAME OF A CORPORATION TO ADVERTISE THEIR PRODUCTS?

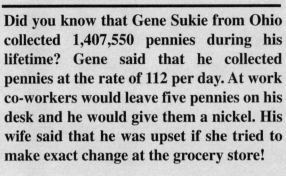

Did you know that Gene Sukie from Ohio collected 1,407,550 pennies during his lifetime? Gene said that he collected pennies at the rate of 112 per day. At work co-workers would leave five pennies on his desk and he would give them a nickel. His wife said that he was upset if she tried to make exact change at the grocery store!

1. WITH THE HELP OF A CALCULATOR, FIND APPROXIMATELY HOW MANY YEARS GENE COLLECTED PENNIES.

2. IF GENE STACKED HIS PENNIES LIKE A CYLINDER, HOW TALL WOULD THE COLUMN BE?

3. SEARCH THE INTERNET TO FIND THE HEIGHT OF THE CN TOWER IN TORONTO AND THE SEATTLE SPACE NEEDLE. COMPARE THESE HEIGHTS WITH GENE'S STACK OF PENNIES!

4. IF GENE SPREAD HIS PENNIES OUT ALONG A STRAIGHT LINE SO THAT THEY TOUCHED, HOW LONG WOULD THE LINE BE?

THINK, TALK, & WRITE ABOUT IT

DO YOU COLLECT ANYTHING?

DO YOU KNOW ANYONE ELSE WHO HAS AN INTERESTING COLLECTION?

Newspaper articles are a rich source for word problems and interesting discussions. If a word problem is worth doing, it is worth thinking, talking, and writing about it!

The four 'clippings' presented in this lesson offer contexts for mathematical discussions that children find engaging. Andras Valezy, a student in a classroom where these word problems were field-tested explained:

What I liked about this math work was that when we were reading the newspaper articles, we didn't just learn about math – we also found out about people.

ANSWERS

<u>Granby</u>

1. $7284

2. It depends on the definition of length and the size of the pool!

<u>Kozy Korner</u>

4200. On average, 5 or 6 cups were sold each day (assuming they were open 365 days a year), so you would think it is a small restaurant, but it is not that small! Maybe the reporter made a mistake.

<u>Traci Dunlop</u> $25,000 divided by 4 = $6250

<u>Sukie</u> 1. Between 34 and 35 years.

2. Seven pennies stack to about one cm or 0.25 inches. So 1,407,550 pennies stack to about 201,079 cm (about 2011m), or about 79,164 inches (6598 feet).

3. The CN Tower is 553m (1814 feet) tall. The Seattle Space Needle is 184m (605 feet) feet tall. Gene's stack of pennies is about 3.6 times the height of the CN Tower and more than 11 times as tall as the Seattle Space Needle!

4. Seven pennies stretch about 13 cm, so 1,407,550 pennies stretch 2,614,021 cm or about 26,140 m or 26 km. This is about 85,301 feet or about 16 miles.

MICHIGAN VS OHIO STATE

IN THIS CLASSIC GAME BETWEEN MICHIGAN AND OHIO STATE SOME OF THE POINTS SCORED ARE MISSING, BUT REPLACED BY FOUR CLUES.

USE THE CLUES TO HELP YOU FILL IN THE MISSING POINTS, THEN ADD TO FIND THE FINAL SCORE.

Team	1st Quarter	2nd Quarter	3rd Quarter	4th Quarter	Total Score
Michigan	7		10		
Ohio		21		7	

CLUES:

1. MICHIGAN SCORED 14 FEWER POINTS THAN OHIO STATE IN THE 2ND QUARTER.

2. FORTY-TWO POINTS WERE SCORED IN THE FIRST HALF.

3. MICHIGAN SCORED THREE MORE POINTS THAN OHIO STATE IN THE 3RD QUARTER.

4. TWENTY-TWO POINTS WERE SCORED IN THE 4TH QUARTER.

Word problems based on quarter-by-quarter football game scores gives students 'word problem' practice in a motivating context.

Having students create their own 'Four Clue' word problems from current games can serve as a great source of word problem review. Students may want to create word problems with more or fewer clues. Note that this activity would be equally appropriate for basketball as well as football.

Answer:

Team	1st Quarter	2nd Quarter	3rd Quarter	4th Quarter	Total Score
Michigan	7	7	10	15	39
Ohio	7	21	7	7	42

NOT
ENOUGH
INFORMATION!

THE FAR SIDE By GARY LARSON

Math phobic's nightmare

Playing Ketchup

Washington has decreed that the best grade of ketchup – the type to be served in its armed forces, schools, and jails – must flow at a rate of three to seven centimeters in 30 seconds; previously the limit was six to eight centimeters per 30 seconds.

At top speed, Grade A tomato ketchup will now take 7 1/2 years to cross Canada at its widest point.

A DAY LATER THIS ARTICLE APPEARED IN THE PAPER.

Ketchup Correction

Top-quality ketchup would take at least 75 years to flow across Canada. An incorrect figure was given yesterday, owing to an error in the thinking process.

WHICH ANSWER IS MORE REASONABLE – 7.5 YEARS OR 75 YEARS?

MISSING INFORMATION: HOW WIDE IS CANADA?

Where's Waldo?

"It takes me about six to eight weeks to complete one picture", the author says. "I have slowed down as time has progressed. I'm pushing myself to the limit, trying to get more happening in each scene."

HOW LONG WOULD IT TAKE TO COMPLETE A WHERE'S WALDO BOOK?

MISSING INFORMATION: HOW MANY PAGES IN A BOOK?

I'M STARVED

THE FAMILY CIRCUS®   By Bil Keane

Copyright 1985
Cowles Syndicate, Inc.

"We'll be away for 41 meals."

HOW MANY DAYS WILL THE FAMILY BE AWAY?

AN ANSWER IS *14 DAYS*.

ALMOST ALL STUDENTS BASED THEIR REASONING ON "THREE MEALS A DAY" — A PIECE OF INFORMATION THEY ADDED TO THE CARTOON.

THE MOST POPULAR ANSWER WAS "*13*", BECAUSE

$$\begin{array}{r} 13 \\ 3\overline{)41} \\ 39 \\ \hline 2 \end{array}$$

OTHER STUDENTS DID NOT IGNORE THE REMAINDER 2.

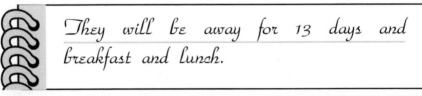

They will be away for 13 days and breakfast and lunch.

They will be away for almost 14 days.

T o many the answer "14" is obviously correct, but thinking problem solvers might have some reservations. People who *take the numb out of numbers* are always questioning their assumptions:

"Does a family always have three meals a day?"

"Will they have three meals the first day of traveling?"

"Could you count 'a meal' for each person eating, so that with five people they would have five meals at a time?"

Maybe problem solving in math should be called "It Depends Math". Depending on your assumptions you will get different answers.

It is often a shock to realize that not everyone looks at a simple statement the way you do. When there is not enough information and it is necessary to assume something, you might expect everyone to make the same assumptions. Not so!

Conversation around the problem to be solved opens minds – not a bad idea as the world rapidly becomes a 'global village'.

CARS! CARS! CARS!

Motorists stuck in 170-kilometer jam

MUNICH, Germany (AP) – Heavy snowfall, icy roads and thousands of holiday travelers combined to produce an unprecedented 170-kilometer (105-mile) traffic jam yesterday in southern Germany.

Police said the traffic jam occurred on the 385-kilometer (240-mile) autobahn linking Frankfurt, Wuerzburg, Nuremberg and Munich.

ESTIMATE HOW MANY CARS YOU THINK WERE IN THE TRAFFIC JAM?

WRITE AN EXPLANATION FOR THIS ANSWER.

 NOT ENOUGH INFORMATION: THE CLIPPING GIVES US NO INFORMATION ON THE LENGTH OF A CAR!

TO HELP YOU MAKE A REASONABLE ESTIMATE, FIND THE LENGTH OF SOME CARS. MAKE SURE THE CARS ARE STOPPED BEFORE MEASURING!

IN MAKING YOUR ESTIMATE WHAT OTHER INFORMATION WOULD BE HELPFUL?

TALK ABOUT IT...

DOES THIS SEEM LIKE A BIG TRAFFIC JAM TO YOU?

TO REALIZE HOW BIG THIS IS, TAKE A MAP AND FIND A TOWN OR CITY WHICH IS ABOUT 170 KILOMETERS FROM WHERE YOU LIVE.

A TYPICAL ANSWER, BASED ON A 5 METER LENGTH OF CAR WAS 34,000. THE ANSWER WAS FOUND BY DIVIDING 170,000 BY 5.

THIS ANSWER CHANGED, HOWEVER, AS THESE DIFFERENT FACTORS WERE LISTED...

How many lanes of traffic?

Does the traffic jam go both ways?

Are the cars bumper to bumper?

Are there other vehicles involved e.g. trucks, motorbikes etc?

Are there cars off to the side of the road?

European cars are smaller!

Once again, it is an education to realize that everybody makes different assumptions in reading a problem and in adding information that is needed. Learning a tolerance for others' ideas is an important part of mathematical literacy.

An interesting follow-up investigation, based on the student's comment on the size of European cars is, "Would there be more than or fewer than 34,000 cars if we agreed European cars are smaller?"

Using simpler numbers and the strategy of drawing a picture helps to convince students that the answer is "more than 34,000 cars"!

In measuring the length of cars the students found that not all cars are the same length, so they had to decide on a reasonable estimate for the length of a car.

> Going outside and actually measuring cars made the problem seem much more real to them– an important ingredient in *taking the numb out of numbers*.

CATS

Kingston, Ont. (CP) – A couple who share their home with 145 cats are a whisker away from winning a continent-wide contest for "Most Cats Under One Roof".

Donna and Jack Wright, who last year were in trouble with city hall for harboring 54 of the frisky felines, have since bolstered their brood to 145 cats and now are among three finalists in the contest sponsored by a U.S. tabloid.

The contest's first prize "will barely pay a day's bills", Jack Wright said.

He said cat food, disinfectant, litter, veterinary care and the help of three housekeepers costs several hundred dollars per week.

To allergy sufferers, it sounds like a nightmare. But Wright, who cuddled a couple of his furry friends during an interview Wednesday, said, "You hardly notice them after a while."

❶. HOW MANY CATS DO DONNA AND JACK HAVE?

❷. HOW MUCH WOULD DONNA AND JACK HAVE TO PAY FOR CAT FOOD EACH WEEK?

NOT ENOUGH INFORMATION
WHAT OTHER INFORMATION DO YOU NEED?
WHERE WOULD YOU FIND THIS INFORMATION?

❸. OVER A YEAR, HOW MUCH WOULD THEY PAY FOR CAT FOOD?

TALK ABOUT IT...

WHAT OTHER PETS DO YOU HAVE OR WOULD LIKE TO HAVE?
CHOOSE ONE OF THESE PETS AND CALCULATE THE WEEKLY AND YEARLY FEEDING COSTS.

❶. DONNA AND JACK HAVE 145 CATS!

SOME THOUGHTS FROM STUDENTS ON QUESTIONS **❷** AND **❸**:

You need to know how much a cat eats and how much cat food costs. You could get the information at Pet Smart or a grocery store or from Donna and Jack!

A can of cat food costs 75 cents. A cat eats half a can a day.

Cat food for 1 cat costs $2.50 a week.
145 x $2.50 = $362.50

I would first have to find out the cost per day and multiply by 365 or I would get the cost per week and muliply it by 52 weeks in the year.

I think they would pay $30,160 a year...But if they won they wouldn't have to pay for the food!

> *I think it would be $580.00 a week for all cats. I think that because at the store they have cat food bags for $3.99 so I rounded to $4.00 and multiplied that by 145 because that's how many cats there are. And I got $580.00 because my cat goes through one bag in a week.*

> *Yes, I have a dog, a cat, a rabbit and fish.*

S tudents usually assume that in a word problem there is just the right amount of information needed to solve the problem. They shuffle the numbers until they get an answer. There is little concern whether or not their answer is

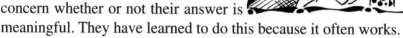

meaningful. They have learned to do this because it often works.

> In life we seldom have exactly the right amount of information. For that reason students need practice with solving problems that have too much or too little information.

Often a newspaper clipping provides the spark for the investigation of other related problems. When students find the cost of feeding their own pets, actual or imagined, it brings a bit of realism to their dreams. Getting the students to link their math to the 'real' world is another step in *taking the numb out of numbers.*

GET A HAIRCUT !

Barber's sign stolen!

Talk about a cut-rate reward! Thomas Anthony, a barber, reported that his new sign had been stolen Monday night.

Now Anthony is offering five years' worth of free haircuts to anyone with information leading to the return of the sign, which was worth $400.

"Twice a month for five years worth of free haircuts to anyone – man or woman – we do both", said the barber.

"Who would want to steal my sign? There are lots better around", said Anthony.

"I don't have any enemies. I've never made an enemy in my life."

HOW MUCH MONEY IS THE BARBER'S OFFER WORTH?

NOT ENOUGH INFORMATION:
WHAT OTHER INFORMATION DO YOU NEED?
WHERE WOULD YOU FIND THIS INFORMATION?

TALK ABOUT IT...

IS THIS A 'GOOD DEAL' FOR THE BARBER?

HERE IS A SAMPLE OF STUDENT RESPONSES TO THE QUESTIONS.

We need to know how much a haircut costs. We could check this out where people get their haircuts.

My haircut costs $5.00 so...

12	24	120
x2	x5	x10
24	120	1200

The barber's offer is worth $1200

This is not a good deal for the barber because he is giving $1,200 and the sign only costs $400."

I think the barber should find how many haircuts it takes to equal $400 and that's how many haircuts he should give away.

182

Depending on the type of barber shop considered, the students returned with different prices for a haircut. Different information led to different answers. The realization that different answers are possible is a sign of *taking the numb out of numbers*.

It is helpful at first to signal that there is not enough information in the clipping to answer the question, because students are not used to this. In time students should decide for themselves that there is not enough information.

DEAL OR NO DEAL

THIS TV GAME SHOW, HOSTED BY HOWIE MANDEL, IS ON NBC TELEVISION. YOU CAN ALSO PLAY IT AS A BOARD GAME OR ON THE INTERNET. IT IS VERY POPULAR AND INVOLVES A COMBINATION OF MATHEMATICAL THINKING AND HUMAN NATURE.

AT THE START OF THE TV PROGRAM **DEAL OR NO DEAL** A LARGE BOARD DISPLAYS THESE 26 DIFFERENT AMOUNTS OF MONEY (CONTAINED IN SUITCASES) THAT A CONTESTANT CAN WIN.

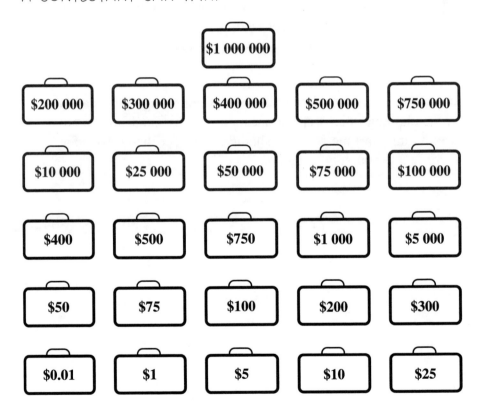

ASK YOUR TEACHER TO EXPLAIN THE RULES. THEN PLAY THIS GAME WITH SLIPS OF PAPER IN ENVELOPES.

The contestant randomly chooses a suitcase without knowing what amount is contained in it. As the game progresses, the banker tries to buy the suitcase from the contestant by making different offers. The contestant opens other suitcases to reveal how much money they hold. These are then eliminated from the game.

Suppose the contestant has eliminated all but the following:

The contestant's suitcase holds one of these amounts. Nobody knows which one!

The Bank then makes an offer of $140,000. The contestant can take that amount and go home (DEAL) or choose to open one of the other suitcases (NO DEAL). If the suitcase that is opened is the one containing $1,000,000 (and the probability of this is 1/5) then the next bank offer will go down because the bank knows the contestant's suitcase must contain less the $1,000,000. But if the contestant selects a suitcase that does not contain $1,000,000 (probability of 4/5) then the bank (fearing that the contestant's suitcase contains $1,000,000) will increase their offer.

The bank offer is always less than or equal to the mean of the amounts left on the board. The Banker's Strategy relies on the contestant's hope that they can defy the odds!

Write on slips of paper the amounts shown on the facing page and place them in envelopes. Explain the rules of Deal or No Deal to your students. Then let the contestant try to win $1,000,000.

Fermi Problems

Enrico Fermi was an Italian physicist who won the Nobel Prize in 1938 for his work on the use of neutrons in controlled chain reactions. A gifted teacher and brilliant scientist, he is known to mathematics educators through his legendary "order-of-magnitude" estimations known as *Fermi problems.*

A Fermi problem seems to have insufficient information for a solution, but it can be solved by making appropriate assumptions and estimates. The classic example of a Fermi problem is one that Enrico Fermi proposed himself, i.e., "How many piano tuners are there in Chicago." The table below presents a sequence of questions and answers that might be used to obtain a reasonable estimate of the number of piano tuners in Chicago.

Question	Answer
What is the population of Chicago?	About 3×10^6
To estimate the number of pianos, should we estimate the number of people or the number of households?	Households rather than individuals tend to own pianos.
About how many households in Chicago?	There may be an average of 4 people per household in Chicago, so the number of households is about $3 \times 10^6 \div 4$.
What proportion of households in Chicago have pianos?	Electric keyboards etc. have probably replaced the piano in many households, so maybe about 1 in 10 households has a piano. That would suggest that there are about $3 \times 10^6 \div 4 \div 10$ or 7.5×10^4 pianos in Chicago.
How many piano tuners are needed to service 75 000 pianos?	Some pianos are never tuned while others are tuned frequently. Suppose this averages out to about one piano tuning per year per piano. Then 75 000 piano tuners are needed. Assuming a piano tuner tunes an average of 3 pianos a day and that the piano tuner works about 200 days per year, the number of piano tuners needed is about 75 000 ÷ 600 or 125.
How many piano tuners are there in Chicago?	There are approximately 125 piano tuners in Chicago.

In *Authentic Learning Activities in Middle School Mathematics: Number and Operation,* Brendan Kelly notes (p. 17):

Because important information is missing, students must ask themselves more questions about what they need to know and about what they already know. Then they must construct a path of estimates that leads from the knowledge that they have to the knowledge they need to acquire. This is a process that we apply in everyday life when we make 'ballpark' estimates of our fuel consumption, bank balances or the time we will need to mark a class test.

These are some Fermi problems which you might like to explore.

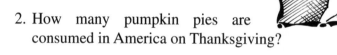

1. How many baseballs are used in a Major League baseball game?

2. How many pumpkin pies are consumed in America on Thanksgiving?

3. How many gas stations are in Canada?

4. How many times does a person blink in a day?

5. How far does the average person walk in a lifetime?

Some approximate answers based on reasonable assumptions made by students are......

1. 100   **2.** 88 million   **3.** 16,500   **4.** 12,000   **5.** 77,000 miles

Which of these estimates seem reasonable (unreasonable) to you?

THE CALCULATOR CORNER

"Look – if you have five pocket calculators and I take two away, how many have you got left?"

With acknowledgements to Punch

The Lottery Scam

RICHMOND, Va. (AP-Special) -A group of 2500 Australian investors spent $5 million trying to win the $27 million jackpot in the Virginia state lottery.

They bought 5 million $1 tickets. Each ticket had a different combination of six numbers chosen from one to 44.

The tickets were bought in bulk from as many as eight grocery or convenience stores that handle lottery sales.

The group ran out of time before they had purchased all possible combinations.

Kids collect pennies...

Julie Chung won't complain if she doesn't see another penny for a long time.

The middle school student spent the last two weeks helping to count $1461.44 worth of pennies.

"We stayed after school until 5:00 p.m. each day," said Chung, who looked peaked before she and her friends had to cart the rolled mass of pennies weighing more than 136 kilograms (300 pounds) to a nearby bank.

The money goes to help needy children!

This expression gives the number of different ticket combinations.

$$\frac{44 \times 43 \times 42 \times 41 \times 40 \times 39}{6 \times 5 \times 4 \times 3 \times 2 \times 1}$$

With a calculator, we find that this is equal to 7,059,052 different tickets. If you bought one ticket every second, 24 hours per day, then the number of days it would take to purchase *all* possible tickets would be:

$$\frac{7,059,052}{60 \times 60 \times 24} \quad \text{or 82 days.}$$

If you placed the pennes end-to-end in a straight line, how long would the line be?

Eight pennies stretch about 15 cm, so a line of 146,144 pennies would be about $(146,144 \div 8) \times 15$ cm long. Using the calculator, we find that this is 274,020 cm or 2.74 km – the length of about 30 football fields!

CAN I HAVE YOUR AUTOGRAPH?

Bateman to sign his name 50 000 times

By John Picton Toronto Star

Don't try to call Robert Bateman next February. He won't be home. Where he *will* be is in a small back room in Venice, Florida, signing his name – perhaps 50,000 times over.

To sounds of the girls whooping it up over coffee and gossip in the hairdressing shop next door, he'll be napping on a camp cot and watching old movies on a rented VCR between 12-hour shifts of putting his signature on more than $9 million worth of his art work.

The print that will be put in front of him 50,000 times is of a pair of mallards and the proceeds will go to the Wildlife Habitat Canada.

They'll sell for $195 each; a special 950-copy executive edition, complete with a gold medallion, will be priced at $2500. Bateman will keep the original.

And what has all this success done for Bob Bateman? Nothing, it seems.

"My lifestyle's exactly the same as when I was a $7,000-a-year teacher", he says.

The former art teacher from Burlington's Nelson High and Lord Elgin High– "I was a full-time teacher until I was 46" (he's now 55) – still remembers those days back in the early 1960's when other teachers could afford to pay the $260 to buy one of his paintings.

He also knows – and regrets – that some of them since have sold those same paintings for as much as $20,000. "But it's a free market system and I have no control over it.

❶. SOME DAY YOU MAY BE FAMOUS SO.... HAVE SOMEONE TIME YOU AS YOU SIGN *YOUR* AUTOGRAPH 25 TIMES ON A PIECE OF PAPER.

❷. CALCULATE HOW MANY HOURS IT WOULD TAKE YOU TO SIGN YOUR AUTOGRAPH 50,000 TIMES!

TALK ABOUT IT...

WOULD BATEMAN TAKE MORE OR LESS TIME THAN YOU TO SIGN HIS AUTOGRAPH 50,000 TIMES? WHY?

WHEN YOU ARE FAMOUS WILL YOU ALWAYS TAKE THE TIME TO SIGN AUTOGRAPHS?

DO YOU HAVE ANY INTERESTING AUTOGRAPHS AT HOME?

WHOSE AUTOGRAPH WOULD YOU REALLY LIKE TO GET?

ONE STUDENT WROTE:

It took me 2 minutes and 24 seconds to sign my name. This is 144 seconds
To sign my name one time would be...
144 ÷ 25 seconds

To sign my name 50,000 times would take...
$$\frac{50,000 \times 144}{25} = 288,000 \text{ seconds}$$
But 288,000 seconds = 288,000 ÷ 60
$$= 4800 \text{ minutes}$$
And...
4800 minutes = 4800 ÷ 60 = 80 hours
So it would take me 80 hours, but that's providing I don't eat or sleep or go to the bathroom. I need an assistant!

AFTER SIGNING HER AUTOGRAPH 25 TIMES ONE STUDENT WROTE...

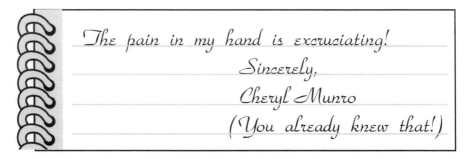

The pain in my hand is excruciating!
Sincerely,
Cheryl Munro
(You already knew that!)

A FEW STUDENTS WOULD REFUSE TO GIVE AUTOGRAPHS, CITING THEIR NEED FOR PRIVACY, BUT MOST WOULD SIGN TO KEEP THEIR FANS HAPPY. AS ONE STUDENT WROTE, "... *without fans nobody goes anywhere.*"

There are three ways to calculate – using mental math, paper and pencil, or a calculator. Each has its place.

This activity invites participation and appeals to students' imaginations. It challenges the common student perception of mathematics as something that is done 'to them'.

Many students thought Bateman would take more time if his name were longer than theirs, and less time if his name were shorter.

Students love to compare the time they take to sign the 25 autographs. Some students suggested a fair way to compare the speed of signing is to find the number of letters each person wrote per second. This is a good follow-up investigation in which a calculator would be very helpful.

A calculator enables students to solve problems involving bigger numbers than they would have confronted in the past. However, a calculator used without understanding is like an excellent basketball shooter taking a shot without knowing where the basket is. By itself, a calculator cannot *take the numb out of numbers.*

CHANNEL SURFING

Most Americans change the
channel about 117,000 times
in their lifetime.
– USA TODAY

IN YOUR LIFETIME WILL YOU CHANGE THE CHANNEL ABOUT 117,000 TIMES, MORE THAN 117,000 TIMES OR LESS THAN 117,000 TIMES?

WRITE A PARAGRAPH TO EXPLAIN YOUR ANSWER.

USE MATHEMATICS TO SUPPORT THIS ANSWER.

THIS IS A SAMPLE OF STUDENT RESPONSES.

117,000 times in a lifetime
÷ 75 years   (average human lifetime)
= 1,560 times per year

1,560 times per year ÷ 365 days a year
= 4.27 times per day

This means that the average person changes channels 4 times per day. I change the channel a lot more than 4 times a day and so I guess I will change it a lot more than 117,000 times in a lifetime.

I'm no couch potato, but I think the answer is way more than 117,000 times. I change the channel 22 times a day. If there are 365 days in a year then you multiply 365 x 22. I got 8030 then I multiply 8030 x 53 because 53 is a lifetime. Your answer will be right there in the calculator — 425,590. That's the number of times I am going to change the channel in 53 years.

If a person flips the channel 10 times a day, by the time the person is 35 she would have changed the channel 127,750 times!

To investigate a problem like this it is helpful to encourage students to...

• Take a wild guess at the answer
• Discuss with friends the various assumptions they might make e.g.

> Number of years people watch T.V.
> The amount of T.V. people watch
> When people channel surf

• List steps in a plan to solve the problem
• Do the math
• Write a convincing solution

Most students concluded that they will change the channel more than 117,000 times. When it came to the arithmetic, some students divided and some multiplied ...All found the calculator a big help.

It is important for students to learn that problems may be solved in different ways! Sharing these different approaches helps *take the numb out of numbers.*

REDUCE, REUSE, RECYCLE

Environmental rules too costly, packing firms say

By Royson James
TORONTO STAR

The people who make packages for food and consumer products say it will be difficult for business to achieve a 20 per cent cut in the amount of packaging by the end of next year.

And some businesses and products could "disappear" because of the planned legislation.

CHOOSE YOUR FAVORITE FOOD WHICH COMES IN A RECTANGULAR SOLID BOX.

DO YOU THINK THE PACKAGING FOR THIS BOX COULD BE REDUCED BY AT LEAST 20%? TO FIND OUT....

- WITH THE BOX FULL OF FOOD, FIND THE TOTAL SURFACE AREA OF THE SIX FACES OF THE BOX.

- NOW OPEN THE BOX. IS THERE A LOT OF EXTRA SPACE INSIDE?

- BY CUTTING AND TAPING, CREATE A NEW RECTANGULAR SOLID BOX WHICH WILL HOLD ALL THE FOOD, BUT HAVE VERY LITTLE SPACE LEFT OVER.

- FIND THE TOTAL SURFACE AREA OF YOUR 'NEW' BOX.
HAS THE NEW BOX REDUCED PACKAGING AT LEAST 20%?

TALK ABOUT IT...WHY MIGHT A COMPANY HESITATE TO CREATE A SMALLER BOX?

ONE STUDENT WROTE THIS COMPLETE SOLUTION.

I chose a 225 gram package of Kraft Dinner
(with macaroni and cheese)

Finding the total surface area:
The 'top' is 3 cm x 9 cm...............27 cm²
The 'bottom' is 3 cm x 9 cm.........27 cm²
One side is 18 cm x 9 cm ....162 cm²
Another side is 18 cm x 9 cm .....162 cm²
One side is 3 cm x 18 cm .... 54 cm²
And the last side is 3 cm x 18 cm = 54 cm²
So the total surface area is...........486 cm²

After cutting the box and squeezing down the
macaroni and the cheese, I taped it to make a
new box. The new surface area is:

The 'top' is 3 cm x 9 cm ....27 cm²
The 'bottom' is 3 cm x 9 cm ....27 cm²
One side is 12 cm x 9 cm ....108 cm²
Another side is 12 cm x 9 cm .....108 cm²
One side is 3 cm x 12 cm ....36 cm²
The last side is 3 cm x 12 cm = 36 cm²
So the 'new' total surface area is 342 cm²
The packaging has been reduced by
486 −342 = 144 cm². This is $^{144}/_{486}$ = 30%.

S tudents often complain that most math problems are irrelevant and uninteresting. However, this newspaper clipping leads to a relevant 'real world' problem.

When this problem is presented in the abstract so that students are given the dimensions of the original box and the height of the food in the box, the students often make false assumptions and get the wrong answer. However, when students work with the actual box and make their own measurements, they are seldom wrong!

It's interesting to note that even though the box loses ⅓ of its height, it doesn't lose exactly ⅓ of its surface area. Examining the box measurements will show why.

> In the long run, students work better in the abstract after they have had an unhurried time working with objects. *Taking the numb out of numbers* takes time!

Some students enjoy using their imagination to create a 'new and improved' box with a different shape!

TIRE FIRE

Huge tire inferno forces 200 to flee

Black smoke billows as 14 million tires burn.

NOW THAT'S A LOT OF TIRES!

HOW MUCH SPACE WOULD THEY OCCUPY?

A VERY CAPABLE STUDENT WROTE:

I measured a tire on a Toyota Camry. The radius was 35 centimeters and the diameter was 70 centimeters, and it was 19 centimeters high when it sat like a doughnut.

Let's assume the tires are stacked 14 high (about the height of a regular room). The height is 14 x 19 cm = 266 cm or 2.66 m.

Then there would be 1,000,000 tires on each level.
Based on a square shape each side will be 1000 tires long.
This is 1000 x 70 cm = 70,000 cm or 700 m.

So the real space occupied by the tires is 700 x 700 x 2.66 = 1,303,400 cubic meters

They would fill a normal sized room of size 700 m x 700 m!

Many interesting ideas surfaced in the solving of this problem...

One student considered stacking the tires in a column. Assuming a height of 19 cm for one tire, then 14,000,000 tires would be 2,660,000 m tall. This is 2660 km tall. This would be the height of 4793 CN Towers stacked on top of one another! (The CN Tower in Toronto is the world's tallest free standing structure at 553 m.)

> Sure this is not a "realistic" problem, but students learn a lot about language by reading fiction. Perhaps they can learn a lot about math by applying it in dramatic contexts.

This wonderful investigation involving measurement, geometry and numbers was made possible by the use of calculators – just another source for *taking the numb out of numbers*.

TWO PROBLEMS ABOUT LIGHTS

❶

ON THE BOX IT SAID THAT THE
LIGHT BULB WAS GOOD FOR
3000 HOURS.

IS THAT A LOT OF TIME OR LITTLE
TIME?

EXPLAIN YOUR THINKING, USING
MATH!

❷

THE AUTHOR WAS DOING A MATH WORKSHOP FOR
TEACHERS IN A HOTEL. HE LOOKED UP AT THE CEILING
AND SAW THIS ARRANGEMENT OF LIGHTS.

```
O O O O O O O O O O O O O O O O O O O O O
O O O O O O O O O O O O O O O O O O O O O
O O O O O O O O O O O O O O O O O O O O O
O O O O O O O O O O O O O O O O O O O O O
O O O O O O O O O O O O O O O O O O O O O
O O O O O                     O O O O O
O O O O O                     O O O O O
O O O O O                     O O O O O
O O O O O                     O O O O O
O O O O O                     O O O O O
O O O O O                     O O O O O
O O O O O                     O O O O O
O O O O O                     O O O O O
O O O O O                     O O O O O
O O O O O                     O O O O O
O O O O O O O O O O O O O O O O O O O O O
O O O O O O O O O O O O O O O O O O O O O
O O O O O O O O O O O O O O O O O O O O O
O O O O O O O O O O O O O O O O O O O O O
O O O O O O O O O O O O O O O O O O O O O
```

FIND AT LEAST TWO DIFFERENT WAYS TO FIND HOW
MANY LIGHTS THERE WERE.

The two problems shown on the opposite page exemplify the difference between problems for which the calculator is needed and those for which it is of no use. The calculator is needed in the first problem to make approximations, but in the second problem, the calculator is of no help in determining the number of lights in the rectangular array.

Student responses to the first problem are shown below.

I think it's a great bulb for my room! Because I leave it on for one hour a day...15 minutes getting up, 20 minutes doing homework, and 25 minutes reading a book. 3000 hours is some bulb! That's a lot of time. So it would last 3000 days which is 3000 divided by 365 which is 8.2 years!

My brother leaves his light on every day. So for him it wouldn't last long! 3000 divided by 24 is 125 days. My parents buy low energy lights to conserve energy...

Bathroom light: Mom: 1 hour, Dad: 1.5 hours, David: 1 hour, Me: 1.5 hours, Grandpa: 1 hour .... Total 6 hours each day ......

One student compared light bulb use in the bathroom, kitchen, living room, and bedroom #1 and bedroom #2!

TRAVELING LIGHT

EACH AIRLINE IN THE USA HAS A LIMIT ON THE MAXIMUM SIZE OF A BAG. IT IS 62 LINEAR INCHES. THIS MEANS IS THAT:

LENGTH + WIDTH + HEIGHT = 62 INCHES.

IF YOUR BAG IS BIGGER, BE PREPARED TO PAY EXTRA!

WHAT WOULD BE THE DIMENSIONS OF A 62-INCH BAG THAT WOULD HAVE THE LARGEST POSSIBLE VOLUME? IT TURNS OUT THAT THE MAXIMUM VOLUME IS FOUND WITH A CUBE SHAPE. I.E. L = W = H.

USE A CALCULATOR TO FIND WHAT MEASURES OF THE LENGTH, WIDTH AND AREA YIELD THE LARGEST PERMISSABLE VOLUME.

AIRLINES LOSE 30 MILLION BAGS

Last year the world's airlines boarded 2 billion passengers who checked 3.7 billion bags. About 30 million bags were lost. The average length of time it takes for a mishandled bag to end up with the owner is 31 hours. About 240,000 bags never reached their owners.

That seems like a lot of bags, but.... maybe it isn't that many!

WHAT PERCENT OF ALL THE BAGS THAT ARE BOARDED ARE LOST? WHAT PERCENT ARE LOST FOREVER?

There are several different ways of computing the percent of bags lost as well as those that are lost forever. The most common process follows this line of reasoning.

Lost: 30,000,000

Processed: 3.7 billion = 3,700,000,000

Fraction lost: 30,000,000 divided by 3,700,000,000

= 3 divided by 370

= 1/ 123 or 0.813%. That is, fewer than 1 bag in 100 is lost.

But most of these bags got back to the owner. So what percent were lost forever?

Forever lost: 240,000

Processed: 3,700,000,000

Fraction forever lost: 240,000 divided by 3,700,000,000 or 1 divided by 15,417. That is, fewer than 0.00648% or fewer than 1 bag in 10,000 is forever lost.

Is that a lot or a little? It's a lot if it's YOUR bag!

Note: This activity is difficult for many students because it requires an understanding of the conversion from decimal fractions to percents that are substantially less than 1. While the calculator is a valuable tool in performing difficult computations, the student needs to understand the relationship between fractions and percents in order to perform the conversions in problems such as this.

Math in Epidemic Proportions

SUPPOSE 1000 PEOPLE ARRIVED IN NEW YORK WITH THE FLU.

ASSUME THAT THE INFECTION RATE IS 2%. THAT IS, EACH PERSON INFECTS 2% OF THE PEOPLE WITH WHOM THEY COME INTO CONTACT.

ASSUME ALSO THAT EACH FLU-STRICKEN PERSON IS IN CONTACT WITH 55 PEOPLE EACH DAY.

COMPLETE THE TABLE BELOW TO SHOW HOW MANY PEOPLE HAVE THE FLU AT THE END OF EACH DAY.

Day	Total Infected (to nearest integer)
1	1000
2	2100
3	4410
4	
5	
6	
7	
8	
9	
10	
11	
12	
13	
14	
15	
16	
17	
18	
19	
20	
21	

SINCE EACH PERSON INFECTS 2% OF THE 55 PEOPLE THEY MEET, THEN EACH PERSON INFECTS (ON AVERAGE) 2% OF 55 OR ABOUT 1.1 PEOPLE.

THEREFORE THE NUMBER OF **NEWLY** INFECTED PEOPLE AT THE BEGINNING OF THE SECOND DAY IS 1.1 TIMES THE NUMBER IN THE FIRST DAY, I.E.1100.

THE **TOTAL** NUMBER OF INFECTED PEOPLE AT THE BEGINNING OF THE SECOND DAY IS THE NUMBER INFECTED AT THE BEGINNING (1000) + THE NUMBER OF NEWLY INFECTED PEOPLE (1100) = 2100.

THE TOTAL NUMBER OF INFECTED PEOPLE AT THE BEGINNING OF THE THIRD DAY IS 2.1 TIMES THE NUMBER AT THE BEGINNING OF THE SECOND DAY = 2.1 X 2100 OR 4410 PEOPLE.

Day	Total Infected (to nearest integer)
1	1000
2	2100
3	4410
4	9261
5	19 448
6	40 841
7	85 766
8	180 109
9	378 229
10	794 280
11	1 667 988
12	3 502 775
13	7 355 828
14	15 447 237
15	32 439 199
16	68 122 319
17	143 056 869
18	300 419 425
19	630 880 792
20	1 324 849 664
21	2 782 184 294

The completed table is shown on the left. Notice how the flu is speading! At the end of 21 days, 2,782,184,294 people have the flu! This helps to explain why there is so much concern about the spreading of the bird flu. What begins as an infection of 1000 people can explode into an infection of almost half of the world's population in three weeks!

This model also explains why employers suggest that employees stay home if they have the flu.

The computation above is based on the (somewhat artificial) assumption that those who are newly infected can transmit the flu within a day to others. It also assumes that those infected on day 1 remain infected on day 21.

Usually students complete the table by calculating the number of newly infected people and forget to add in the number who are currently infected and may go on to infect others. When they neglect to account for those who are currently infected, they erroneously conclude that only 6723 people have the flu.

Have students explore this problem when the infection rate is different from 2% or the number of contacts is different from 55.

THE TOP 10 PROBLEM SOLVING STRATEGIES

Children have a great deal of difficulty solving word problems in mathematics. When we administered the following problem to a large number of students, we found some interesting patterns in student answers.

> Pam has 4 pictures. There are 3 cars and 5 trees in each picture.
>
> Which expression gives the total number of trees in the pictures?
>
> **A.** $4 + 5$ **B.** 4×3 **C.** 4×5 **D.** $4 + 3 + 5$

Which answer do you think most 3rd and 4th grade students have chosen, A,B, C, or D? That's right, D.

Why do most students choose an answer which makes no sense whatsoever?

Reasons include...

- Being mislead by the word 'total'

- Feeling they have to use all the numbers in the word problem

- Feeling the time pressure to get a quick answer

- Reading difficulties

Taking the time to use the strategy of 'drawing a picture' would increase the chances of success for most students. Observe the pictures on the following page and note how the picture captures all the information in the first two sentences of the word problem. Then the answer to the question, "What expression gives the total number of trees in the pictures?" becomes more obvious, i.e., 4×5.

Listed below are:

THE TOP 10 PROBLEM SOVING STRATEGIES

1. Draw a picture or diagram.

2. Use objects.

3. Act out a situation.

4. Use trail and error ... Guess and check.

5. Reduce to a simpler related problem. Substitute smaller numbers.

6. Work backwards.

7. Make an organized list or table.

8. Look for a pattern and use inductive reasoning.

9. Use logical reasoning.

10. Use common sense

CREATING AN ENVIRONMENT AT HOME AND AT SCHOOL FOR...
...TAKING THE NUMB OUT OF NUMBERS

Taking the Numb out of Numbers seems to happen when the following conditions apply...

SUCCESS, NOT FAILURE
FUN, NOT FEAR
EXCITEMENT, NOT BOREDOM
ACTIVITY, NOT PASSIVITY
PLAYFULNESS, NOT REGIMENTATION
EXTENSIONS, NOT LIMITS
PATTERN SEEKING, NOT JUST RECOGNITION
CO-OPERATION, NOT JUST COMPETITION
SURPRISES, NOT JUST ROUTINES
QUESTIONING, NOT JUST ANSWERING
UNDERSTANDING, NOT JUST MEMORIZING
TALKING, NOT JUST LISTENING

Taking the Numb out of Numbers is also observed when these verbs are frequently used...

DO, PREDICT, EXPLORE, REASON, GUESS, ANTICIPATE, ESTIMATE, COMMUNICATE, CONNECT

Taking the Numb out of Numbers also occurs when these questions are often heard...

WHY? WHAT IF? IS THAT REASONABLE?, DOES THAT MAKE SENSE?

What is the math environment in your home or classroom?

A GOOD EXAMPLE OF TAKING THE NUMB OUT OF NUMBERS

A school bus holds 36 students. 1128 students are being bused to Harbourfront.

HOW MANY BUSES ARE NEEDED?

To solve this problem most students divided 1128 by 36 obtaining 31.333..., and then claimed that 31.3 buses were needed. Others obtained a quotient of 31 with a remainder of 12, and concluded that 31 buses were needed. These students saw this as an arithmetic exercise in division. They didn't make sense of the math.

Other students answered "32 buses". They used their common sense to interpret the results of their arithmetic. Some of these students used multiplication, not division, to get the answer. They tried 10 buses; i.e., 36 × 10 = 360 and deduced that they needed more buses. Then they tried 30 buses; i.e., 36 × 30 = 1080 – still not enough buses! Eventually they settled on 32 buses. They were willing to play with the numbers and use a good problem solving strategy called "guess-and-check". Although this approach took more time, the problem is not intended as a timed arithmetic drill. These students made sense of the math.

One student answered, "They will need 31 buses and there will be 12 students who will not have a seat on the buses." No one else had thought of the problem in this way! This is an example of good thinking leading to a correct yet surprising answer!

When this last solution was discussed with the class, one student said, "You need only one bus!" Use it as a shuttle. Take 36 students to Harbourfront, return and take 36 more etc.– 32 trips, The rest of the students then gave arguments for 2 or 3 or any number of buses!! A simple division exercise became a wonderful adventure in *taking the numb out of numbers*.

215

THE NATIONAL COUNCIL OF TEACHERS OF MATHEMATICS AND TAKING THE NUMB OUT OF NUMBERS

We can teach them what they need to run a machine or develop a marketing plan. What is killing us is having to teach them to read, compute,... and to think.

–Louis Gerstner, CEO, IBM
Education Summit, March 1996

The *National Council of Teachers of Mathematics* (NCTM) has been a leader in recognizing and addressing the high levels of innumeracy in North American society. In 1989, the NCTM published *Curriculum and Evaluation Standards for School Mathematics.* In 2000, they published the sequel to this document titled, *Principles and Standards for School Mathematics* which became the blueprint for the design of mathematics curricula in the early 21st century. Embedded in that document is a vision of mathematics education that embraces at all grade levels, ten overarching themes or "standards". Included among these ten standards are the following five that identify the major components of a complete mathematics program.

❶. Problem Solving
❷. Reasoning and Proof
❸. Communication
❹. Connections
❺. Representation

Taking the Numb out of Numbers not only endorses these standards, but has been designed to address them by presenting activities that have been successfully field-tested with students. On the following page, I provide a more detailed discussion of these standards as they are embodied in the activities of this book. In this way, I hope the help you, the teacher, to implement lessons that will excite, engage and stimulate your students as they acquire the mathematical literacy so vital in the information age.

❶. Problem Solving

Problem solving goes beyond the word problems you remember from your school days. Numeracy, literacy and thinking are key components of today's problem solving. *Taking the Numb out of Numbers* is full of interesting, relevant and fun problems to solve. It also provides realistic strategies for solving these problems. Often *Taking the Numb out of Numbers* involves computation – mental, pencil-and-paper, or with a calculator. To *take the numb out of numbers* a person must not only know how to add, subtract, multiply, and divide, but also know which of these operations to choose in solving a particular problem. Checking answers for "reasonableness" and playing with the numbers in a variety of ways, are also manifestations of *taking the numb out of numbers.*

❷. Reasoning and Proof

Often there is not just one answer to a problem. Different assumptions in reading and solving the problem will lead to different results. If the thinking and the reasoning are correct, then it's OK to have different answers. *Taking the Numb out of Numbers* stresses the mix of language, math and thinking!

As students progress through the grades, they will acquire an increasingly more sophisticated idea of what constitutes a proof. In the early grades, proof is about plausibility, while in the later grades, proof becomes more formal. Eventually students learn how to reason deductively from basic axioms.

❸. Communication

Through speaking and listening, reading and writing, students communicate their questions and their findings in mathematics. Brainstorming, cooperative learning, writing in journals and portfolios have become effective means of encouraging communication in the math classroom. The activities in *Taking the Numb out of Numbers,* are best done with others. This encourages communication and develops the ability to express mathematical ideas verbally. When these activities are pursued at home, they stimulate exciting family discussions.

❹. Connections

The complaint most often heard from students about their study of mathematics is that they don't understand how it is relevant to their world. Completing pages of arithmetic operations or solving artificial word problems are perceived as routine drills that are devoid of any particular purpose except to generate grades for a report card. However, all the activities and problems in *Taking the Numb out of Numbers* are based on real newspaper clippings or popular television shows – a wonderful connection to the world outside school!

❺. Representation

The new technologies such as graphing calculators, graphing software, spreadsheets and data management tools enable students to represent and interpret information in a variety of different ways. Converting information from one format to another is becoming a vital part of mathematical literacy. For this reason, you will see a number of tables, graphs, visual displays and Internet web sites presented in the pages of this book. In this way, I hope to help you capture the richness of our quantitative world in its many manifestations. Your students will be the beneficiaries of the personal innovation that you bring to the enhancement and implementation of these activities.

WHO SHOULD READ THIS BOOK?

- For parents, teachers and kids from 5th grade through 9th grade – it's a book to be discussed between the generations.

- For those who are looking for a fun-filled, thoughtful and interactive math book.

- For those who believe in linking laughter, learning and math.

- For those who like math and for those who wish they did...For those who already make sense out of math and for those who would like to make sense out of math.

- For those who are looking for enriching problem solving materials

and ...

- For those who want to TAKE THE NUMB OUT OF NUMBERS!!

Exciting Internet Sites for Math Activities

The Internet has a large number of sites that offer free mathematics activities, puzzles and problems that you can use in the classroom. In some cases, these activities can be printed out and distributed as is to your students. In other cases, the puzzles are interactive and students work on the computer, gaining instant feedback as they work. I invite you to explore the sites given below as invaluable resources that will reduce your workload and yet enhance the classroom experience for your students.

Ask Dr. Math (The Math Forum)   http://mathforum.org/dr.math/

This is a wonderful site (created by Drexel University) that enables students to ask questions of Dr. Math and receive answers. Accessing the link titled, "Elementary School," enables students to visit previously asked questions and answers are posted on this site. Clicking on the "puzzles" link, brings the student to:

http://mathforum.org/library/drmath/sets/elem_puzzles.html

where he or she will find lots of interesting puzzles and problems.

edHelper   http://www.edhelper.com/math.htm

This site has a comprehensive offering of worksheets and exercises that require that the student sign in. However, the home page has a variety of links that enable you to access (without signing in) a variety of mathematical topics including puzzles located at:

http://www.edhelper.com/runaway_math_puzzle.htm

Education Place (Houghton Mifflin)
http://eduplace.com/math/brain/

Each week, a " brain teaser" word problem is presented on this site for various grade levels. A useful source of word problems and puzzles in the "brain teaser" category. A link to the archives gives problems from previous weeks and their solutions.

Amusing Facts.com   http://www.amusingfacts.com/brain/

There are several hundred brain teasers on this site, (many of them are old classics) and most of them are mathematical although some might qualify as riddles. Nevertheless, this is a plentiful source of teasers that will engage your students at all grade levels.

Math.com   http://sudoku.math.com/

If you were excited by the Sudoku puzzles you found in this book and you want more, you can find them on this site. Math.com gives five new Sudoku puzzles every day and has an on-line puzzle that enables the student to insert numbers and find their errors as they progress.

Who's Counting (ABC News)
http://abcnews.go.com/Technology/WhosCounting/

If you're looking for some topical articles with a mathematical context, you will find this a fascinating site. Interesting problems, paradoxes and mathematical gems are presented by Professor John Allen Paulos (author of *Innumeracy* and other popular books about mathematics) in a style that is entertaining and informative. Some of the topics are at a high school level, but many are appropriate for elementary school students.

USA Today   http://usatoday.com/news/snapshot.htm

The USA Snapshots that you've seen throughout this book come from the *USA Today* newspaper, but they are available at this Web site, where you may also contribute to a survey by answering a question that is posed. These USA snapshots are a wonderful way to introduce surveys into your classroom activities and to stimulate discussions involving statistics and the collection of data.

Data Sources for Creating Real-World Problems

The word problems in this book used information from a variety of sources. Among them are the following Web sites that you can use to give your word problems currency and perceived relevance.

Census in Schools – U.S. Census Bureau
http://www.census.gov/dmd/www/teachers.html

A rich set of population and demographic data from US Census Bureau. Excellent lesson plans and student activities are also provided.

Treasury Direct –U.S. Treasury Dept.
http://www.treasurydirect.gov/NP/BPDLogin?application=np

Gives the U.S. public Debt to the penny for any particular time period. Great for having students work with large numbers. Also a good source for pie graphs. This site also contains important interest rate data.

U.S. National Debt Clock
http://www.brillig.com/debt_clock/

Gives the total national debt and provides an opportunity to compare with the Treasury Direct information.

The U.S. Mint   http://www.usmint.gov:80/kids/teachers/lessonPlans/lessonSummary.cfm?subjectId=1

A delightful collection of math games and activities built in the context of money and coins.

Classic Fermi Questions
http://mathforum.org/workshops/sum96/interdisc/classicfermi.html

A source of two model Fermi problems. Shows the solution to two classic Fermi Problems. Click on the *Fermi Questions Library* link to get more Fermi Problems. The URL for this library is:
http://mathforum.org/workshops/sum96/interdisc/fermicollect.html